D0437529

JAY McGRAW's
LIFE STRATEGIES
FOR DEALING WITH
BULLIES

ALSO BY JAY McGRAW

Closing the Gap

Daily Life Strategies for Teens

Life Strategies for Teens

Life Strategies for Teens Workbook

The Ultimate Weight Solution for Teens

JAY McGRAW's LIFE STRATEGIES FOR DEALING WITH BULLIES

Jay McGraw

Illustrated by Steve Björkman

ALADDIN

New York   London   Toronto   Sydney

The anecdotes in this book are used to illustrate common issues and problems, and do not necessarily portray specific people or situations. With the exception of a few people that were the subject of prior media coverage, no real names have been used.

ALADDIN

An imprint of Simon & Schuster Children's Publishing Division

1230 Avenue of the Americas, New York, New York 10020

Copyright © 2008 by Jay McGraw

All rights reserved, including the right of reproduction in whole or in part in any form.

Aladdin and related logo are registered trademarks of Simon & Schuster, Inc.

Book design by Jessica Sonkin

The text for this book is set in Adobe Garamond Pro.

The illustrations for this book are rendered in pen and ink.

Manufactured in the United States of America

First Aladdin hardcover edition October 2008

2 4 6 8 10 9 7 5 3 1

CIP data for this book is available from the Library of Congress.

ISBN-13: 978-1-4169-7473-4

ISBN-10: 1-4169-7473-3

FIRST EDITION

To my beautiful wife,
Erica, who makes me smile a little bigger
each and every day. You are so special.
I love you.
And to
my mom and dad for teaching me
how to respect myself and others.
And to
my brother, Jordan, who always has my back.
And to
Grandma, because you are such an amazing person!
And to
all of you who have stood up to a bully
and gone on to tell your story.

JAY McGRAW's
LIFE STRATEGIES
FOR DEALING WITH
BULLIES

BULLIES HAVE BEEN A HUGE PROBLEM for as long as there has been any kind of society. Physical intimidation, teasing, and taunting are all ways bullies isolate victims, and that isolation is a key weapon in the bully's arsenal. Once limited to the playground, classroom, and any place or time that a bully could escape the watchful eye of protective authority figures, bullying has now crept into many other areas as the bullies of today's generation find new ways to bring misery to their victims. Thanks to the wide reach of the Internet, the loss of social connections in our highly transient society, and perhaps a growing numbness to violence, the bully's "playground" has gotten a whole lot bigger, and the methods of domination and exploitation are much more varied and even more invisible to the protector's eye.

It used to be that kids knew they could find some relief from pain and humiliation and an escape from harassment in their own homes. But via the Internet, "keyboard bullies" can come right into your home, penetrating this once safe haven. Some of the worst bullying is now done online via websites such as Facebook, MySpace, and other "social" online gathering places, as well as through e-mails and text messages to cell phones. Officials in some states have even proposed laws to make cyberbullying a criminal offense because it has become such a problem.

If you are being bullied in the real world, the virtual world, or both, and feel that there is no escape, this book brings a message of hope and important strategies for protecting yourself and your peace of mind. My son Jay has been passionately involved in efforts to eradicate bullying for many years. He has written this book to help you know that you don't deserve to be picked on, and that there are proven methods for stopping bullies in their tracks and shutting down this exploitation once and for all.

This book will not only show you how to help yourself, but it will also tell you how to ask for help in the *right* way from the *right* people. Bullying should no longer be written off or excused as a "part of growing up." You can ignore bullies, but they will not go away. They don't disappear just because you have your eyes shut, look the other way, or turn the other cheek. And Jay makes it clear in this book that it is up to all of us to make certain that those bullies who repeatedly intimidate, harass, and physically abuse others are stopped and not allowed a place in our lives or the lives of others.

Since I'm the father of the author, let me address the

parents who pick up this book; or let me offer you this to share with your parents:

Bullying is not kids just being kids.

Bullying is not something that kids should be left to work out for themselves.

Being bullied can change your child in long-term and devastating ways.

Jay has written a serious and important book about a serious and important social problem, and it is packed with solid, practical advice that may be just what you need to turn things around. I am proud that he has taken this subject on and feel so blessed to be his dad. I hope this book will help give kids the opportunity to grow up "bully-free" and parents the opportunity to watch their children grow into adulthood and be as proud of them as I am of my son.

—Dr. Phil

TABLE OF CONTENTS

INTRODUCTION

It's Craig's first day at his new elementary school. He doesn't know any of the other kids in his sixth-grade class, and he's very quiet, even shy. He doesn't make friends easily. Most of the other kids have attended the school for two or three years and know one another pretty well. There are some really tight groups.

As they head out for recess, most of the kids ignore Craig. He wanders over to a set of monkey bars and begins to play by himself. But not all of the kids are busy doing something else. Danny, a very tall, thickset sixth grader, is watching Craig closely. He heads toward the monkey bars where Craig is swinging.

Craig barely notices Danny as he's dangling from the monkey bars. But then he feels Danny brush past his foot.

"Hey, you kicked me!" Danny screams.

"No, I didn't," says Craig. "I was just hanging there." He drops down.

Danny walks up closer to Craig and gets in his face. "You kicked me, so that must mean you think you're tough, huh? You think you're tough, punk?"

Craig stutters, backs away, and trips. Danny raises his foot as if he's going to stomp Craig. Craig covers his face. Danny laughs and walks off.

Craig stands up, relieved, hoping that that's the last time he'll have to deal with Danny. But it won't be. In fact, it's only a start to what turns out to be a nightmare month and a half for Craig.

Every day after that, Danny does something to frighten Craig. He balls up his fist and acts like he is going to hit Craig. He bumps into Craig while walking to his seat at the lunch table— every day. He pokes Craig in the back of his head over and over while they're in line heading into gym. And every now and then, Danny gets right up in Craig's face and warns him, "If you go whining to the teachers, I'm really going to get you, punk."

Craig is a small kid, and he doesn't want to tell his parents; he doesn't want them to worry. And he's not sure his teachers

2

will be able to help. After being in the class for a few weeks, he still hasn't made any friends. He is miserable. And every day, Danny tries harder to make it worse.

STOPPING BULLIES: IT STARTS WITH YOU

Unfortunately, this sort of scenario plays out on far too many playgrounds and in far too many parks around the country. Every day thousands of students are picked on, harassed, and insulted in all kinds of ways. And we're not just talking about a shove or a poke.

Each year preteens are sent to the hospital with broken bones, concussions, and other wounds as a result of being attacked by bullies. In even worse cases, some have been shot or stabbed or even murdered. Bullying is taking a huge toll.

But even when the scars aren't physical, bullying can do some heavy damage. Online bullying is the new rage nowadays, with bullies turning to computers to do their dirty work. Where once bullying could at least be limited to the playground, today you can be hounded and tormented even in your own home.

Online, in school, at home—to some of you, the bullying can seem like it's threatening to swallow you whole. And in some sad cases, it does. Suicides and attempted suicides are up, and our airwaves and headlines are filled with news

about kids, teens, and young adults committing horrible acts as a result of uncontrolled rage, sadness, and depression over being picked on and left out.

Bullying is worse than it's ever been, and the results seem to be getting sadder, more painful, every day. I'm tired of reading about fourteen-year-olds killing themselves because they were tired of being picked on day after day after day. I don't want to hear any more TV news reports about a thirteen-year-old taking too many pills or a twelve-year-old showing up at school with a knife because he's scared and mad about being slapped by a fourteen-year-old on the playground.

But I'm not just going to close my newspaper or turn off my TV. I think this is a problem that you—each and every one of you—can stop on your own. YOU have the power to end bullying right now. That's why I'm writing this book, as part of my larger effort to try and put an end to bullying in our schools and in our neighborhoods. As I'm always telling people, we're all responsible for keeping one another safe. You owe it not only to yourself, but also to your friends and classmates, people who may be weaker than you or who might not be able to stand up for themselves.

And if you're the one who's getting bullied, you owe it to yourself to stop it from happening again. And you can bring it to an end if you're willing to take the necessary steps. I'm not saying it's going to be quick or easy. I'm not saying that you have to do it alone. I'm not even saying that you won't be scared.

BUT YOU CAN DO IT—AND YOU HAVE TO!

Of course, the first thing you have to do is get real about your situation. This is the first step to handling almost any challenge. In my book *Life Strategies for Teens*, I talk about "Life Laws," ideas that are designed to help people live better. One of the first lessons in that book is what I told you at the start of this paragraph: Get real about it.

In your case, getting real about it may mean that you have to first accept that you are being bullied. You may not like the idea that it is happening to you, and I understand that. None of us wants to think of ourselves as a victim. But if you're being bullied, just saying to yourself that you don't want it to happen isn't enough. It's not just a matter of what you want here. It's also about having a good plan, the support you need, and the willingness to do what it takes to achieve your goal. But first and foremost, you have to get real about what is happening!

Don't downplay bullying. Some people might think of it as just "part of being a kid." Ask me and I'll tell you that that sort of thinking stinks. Being bullied is very common—but it's not normal, and it is certainly not okay. Being kept in fear by a person or some group or clique is no way to go into your teen years or young adulthood. And it will leave scars on you that can last a lifetime—even if those scars are on your heart rather than on your body. Growing up in Dallas, I saw some pretty bad cases of bullying, and I always worked hard not to be a bully, but also not to be a victim. What I'm telling you here aren't just some ideas I've come up with out of thin air. These are strategies that have worked for other people and will work for you if you let them.

I've traveled all over the country talking to people about what it's like for them, and I'm saddened and surprised that so many young people have to deal with bullies but don't really have any resources they feel they can use to figure out what to do.

I know this book will help you if will just try out my ideas. I'm not saying that I have all the answers here or that everything I suggest is going to work in every situation. People's lives are all different. But what I've tried to do is offer some ideas about what's really behind bullying and how to start thinking about putting an end to it in your life or in the life of someone you know.

I've drawn on many of the lessons I've learned from my dad. And even though many of these lessons would work in other areas of your life too, I have tried to explain them so that they deal specifically with bullying and how it affects us all.

I'm also pretty sure that along the way, you can find ways to help yourself become a better you, be more confident, be able to make more friends, and become more positive about yourself and life and the road ahead. Bullying can take this kind of joy out of your life if you let it happen. I want this book to be a reminder to you of your value and importance in the world and why you cannot afford to let a bully take that away from you (or from the rest of us).

But you don't have to be the victim of a bully to get something out of this book. Maybe something you read here will help you help someone else. Heck, maybe you're even a bully yourself and you don't really want to be. (And you know what? You shouldn't want to be, because being a bully is really uncool.) I want the conversation you'll find here to give you some ideas that you can use to help bring the bullying to a stop.

And we've definitely got to try to stamp out bullying anywhere we find it. Because with so many students hurting and dying from bullying, y'all can't afford to let it get any worse. It is time to put an end to bullying, and that starts with you.

1
WHAT IS BULLYING?

Kenny, age eleven: *I'm in elementary school, and there's this kid named Ricky who picks on me every other day, for no reason at all. I don't even see it coming sometimes. Some days I'll just be walking through the hall at school, alone, minding my business, and he shows up out of nowhere and just starts shoving me, yelling and calling me bad names: "Hey, stupid." "What's up, moron?" "Go kill yourself, you jerk."*

It wouldn't be so bad if all he did was call me names. But he does a lot more. Ricky is, like, four inches taller than me and heavier, so it's pretty easy for him to push me around whenever he wants to. And he wants to a lot. He trips me, punches me, and slaps me at least twice a week.

I probably should tell the teachers or my folks about what is going on, but Ricky always says that he'll "really kick my butt" if I tell. So I stay quiet. I think I remember the assistant principal at our school pulling Ricky into his office once after he heard Ricky calling me a bad name, but even that didn't seem to stop him. He just became more careful about picking on me when other teachers weren't around.

I want to stand up to Ricky or do something else to get him to leave me alone. But the truth is, I never do anything. The only way I'm getting away from Ricky is because my family is moving to another town. But what if there's another Ricky in my next town?

As alone as Kenny felt when he was getting picked on, the sad truth is that what happened to him happens to kids all over America. In elementary school bathrooms and hall-ways. In junior high locker rooms and playgrounds. Even at home. Bullying is everywhere these days, spreading through almost every method of communication there is. And it's hurting the lives of more young people than we realize.

Maybe, in one way or another, it's even happened to you.

Now maybe you're thinking, "Hold up, Jay, I never let

another kid push me around like that guy. And if someone tries, I know I'd stand up for myself. Or at least I'd go to a teacher or my parents or some friends. No way would I let that happen."

Well, if that's the case, good for you. Obviously, no one should stand for being shoved down and slapped. But standing up against a bully isn't always an option; sometimes the bullies are simply too big to do that.

Also, if you think that's all there is to bullying, you're wrong. Many people think of bullying as little more than a mean shove here or a mean-spirited pinch or punch there. But the truth is, bullying has never been that simple—and it's definitely getting worse for a lot of you.

Small, mean acts are still part of bullying. But that's not all there is to it these days, not by a long shot. Increasingly, physical bullying is taking the form of more serious crimes. Children, preteens, even teens are being beaten up by large groups, and some have been really hurt—in some cases killed—with weapons. Bullying has never been a laughing matter. Nowadays it can also be a life-or-death one.

Of course, bullying isn't just about physically attacking another person either. Bullying comes in other forms too. For almost every form of communication, there are ways to use it to put down, frighten, or hurt others. You can be picked on by others in relationships, through group pressure, in online exchanges in chat rooms, through text messages, and on message boards. You can be bullied when others spread rumors and lies. And in each case, the bullying can leave some pretty deep and long-lasting scars.

Bullying is a horrible thing, and it happens way too much. Some researchers have said that up to 90 percent of children in elementary school have bullied in some way or another—90 percent! Sure, you may not have been bullied like Kenny, whose story we told earlier in this chapter. But chances are that you probably have been picked on by some other person. Or you certainly know somebody who has.

> **FAST FACT**
>
> In the United States alone, bullying affects more than five million students in grades six through eleven.
> One out of seven students has reported being bullied.
> *(Source: National Institutes of Health, 2000)*

So let's keep it real, y'all. Kenny is not "weaker" or "worse" than other people. Students who get bullied are everywhere—they may be your buddy or your brother. Or you. And most important of all, they are people who don't deserve to have anyone call them names or push them around.

I want to take a few minutes to go over the various types of bullying that students like you have to deal with these days.

Before I do, let me just remind you that these definitions are there to help you understand the different types of bullying you can face. But *all* bullying is bad, no matter what type. So don't think I'm trying to compare one form of bullying to another. One type is just as bad as any other, so you should try to avoid or stop any of the various forms of bullying you see happening.

Let me emphasize that last line again, just to make sure you understand me: *You should try to stop any form of bullying you see.* As you read this book, you'll find out more about how to do this.

As I'll discuss later, I firmly believe that when it comes to bullying, there are no innocent bystanders. We all have to stand up and stop bullying wherever we see it. Whether it is happening to us or someone else, we still have a responsibility to stop it. When you see bullying, report the bully to a parent, a teacher, or someone else in authority. Stand with the kid who's being picked on, to let him know that you won't tolerate bullying in any way.

One of the main reasons a lot of bullying goes on is because not enough people who witness bullying—in any of the forms that I'll discuss next—are willing to help bring it to an end.

Also, I'm not saying this is the complete list. Maybe

13

there are other forms of bullying you've seen or had to go through. Hopefully, some of the ideas we will discuss later in this book will help you handle those situations. Meanwhile, let's take a look at some common types of bullying.

PHYSICAL BULLYING

Connor's parents didn't notice that their ten-year-old son had been acting strangely in recent weeks. Some days he'd hurry past them, go into his room, and not come out for the rest of the day. He was jumpy and nervous. He got angry more quickly than usual. He was even losing weight—even though he kept asking them for more and more money for lunch.

Finally Connor's dad followed him into his bedroom one day after school. Connor tried to hide his face, but his dad saw something that shocked him: a large bruise on his cheek. At first Connor wouldn't talk to his father, but he finally told his dad that a bully at school was beating him up for his lunch money every day. The boy, a year older and several pounds heavier, would meet Connor at the front door of the school, just before they went into class. "Hey, squid! Whatcha got for me today?" Connor would usually hand over the money to avoid a beating, he told his dad. But many days that didn't work. The bully still pushed Connor and punched him. "Because I feel like it," the bigger kid would say.

Connor said that he hadn't told his father before because he was too embarrassed. He was also afraid that the bully would pick on him even worse if he told someone. But now that his father had seen the bruise, Connor just couldn't hold back the truth anymore.

Connor's story is about the kind of bullying that many people think of as typical bully behavior. The stereotypical bully is the really big kid who gets pleasure out of pounding on smaller peers. And in some cases, this is true.

But that's not the only kind of bullying there is. Physical attacks take place a lot among young people. Physical bullying includes punching, kicking, slapping, shoving, pinching, biting, scratching, or hair pulling. People often think of larger students as bullies, because they think it would be easier for someone bigger to get away with harming someone smaller. But the truth is, physical bullying can come from kids who are smaller, too. Many times bigger kids are bullied by smaller kids who view larger, overweight classmates as odd or threatening.

Physical bullying also includes the mishandling, damaging, or destroying of your property. You may have had your books knocked into puddles, your book bags tossed onto school

rooftops, or your belongings ripped right out of your arms. Maybe you've had your jewelry taken, your bicycle trashed, or your locker damaged. Destroying property is one more way that a bully can show physical power over you.

Bullying can lead to some serious physical harm as well. Bullies have broken limbs, left scars that won't ever go away, and, in some of the worst cases, even nearly killed their victims. In other cases, bullying has gotten so bad that it has led the bullied student to kill him- or herself!

All types of bullying are done to hurt your feelings. But

16

physical bullying goes a step past that. It's about hurting your feelings *and* your body.

You may have heard the line, "Sticks and stones may break my bones, but words will never hurt me." Well, the truth is that sometimes words can hurt just as much as actions. And with physical bullying, not only do you get the emotional pain that comes from being the target of bullies, but you can get your body hurt too.

I wouldn't say physical bullying is "worse" than some of the other forms of bullying we're going to discuss in this chapter. But I would say that it's the one form of bullying that is sure to affect you on the outside as well as on the inside.

VERBAL BULLYING

Deborah hates to see Victoria coming. Because whenever Victoria shows up, Deborah knows that she is going to be insulted. Victoria is a popular sixth-grade student who thinks it is really funny to insult Deborah. She makes fun of Deborah's clothes and shoes, calling them "tacky" and "cheap." She talks about Deborah's hair and eyes, calls her dumb and fat and a "cross-eyed cow." And Victoria's friends treat Deborah the same way.

They never hit Deborah, but their words leave bruises

17

on Deborah's feelings all the time. Many days Deborah goes home and just sits in her room and cries from all the pain the girls' words cause her. There are even some days when Deborah doesn't make it home before she starts to cry. If Deborah can't make it home, she goes to a girls' bathroom in her school and stands in the corner sobbing quietly, which only makes her more vulnerable to being picked on. And sometimes, after she cries for a long time, she'll walk out of the bathroom and turn the corner, only to find Victoria and her friends standing nearby, ready to insult her some more. On those days Deborah leaves school early, sometimes not even bothering to tell her teachers she is sick. The truth is, she really hurts because of the mean things Victoria and her friends have said.

Verbal bullying means the bully is using words (rather than fists) to attack you. Whenever someone calls you bad names all the time, or tries to insult you with words in other ways, that's verbal bullying.

Unlike physical bullying, verbal bullying doesn't always need the bully to be around you to actually do the bullying. Verbal bullying can mean spreading rumors, gossip, and lies (or even embarrassing private truths) about you or your family or friends. Verbal bullying is often designed

not only to hurt the victim, but also to change how other people see that person.

Verbal bullying may be one of the easier forms of bullying to get away with. And because it leaves no scars that people can see, it's harder for some people to recognize when it happens. Verbal bullying hurts a person's feelings and self-esteem and can leave scars that last for years—for a lifetime, even. Many people who are the victims of verbal bullying have a hard time ever truly liking themselves again or feeling good about the things they accomplish.

Verbal bullying is done to make you appear "strange" to other people—and even to yourself. Bullies aim their insults at things about you that make you distinct from others, whether it's your clothes, your voice, your skin color, your weight, or anything else.

One of the most common areas bullies target is your looks. You're in the early years in your life, and you're still growing into your body. Not everyone is growing at the same rate, in all the same areas, and to the same size. Sometimes it seems like bullies can smell when you're insecure about something physical, and they will use that insecurity to make up insults to hurt your feelings. They will ride you day in and day out about that thing. If you're overweight, it's "Hey, Dumbo," every time the bully sees you. If you wear glasses, you're a "four-eyed geek."

Of course, we know that there are even worse names that some kids get called. Labeling people because they come from a certain racial or ethnic background is a common and disgusting form of verbal bullying. Girls get picked on by boys who see them as weaker or not as smart. (Which is totally untrue!)

Verbal bullying can hurt as much as physical bullying and shouldn't be thought of as "just words" that you're supposed to simply overlook. I encourage you to be strong enough to know that mean things bullies say about you aren't true. You must realize that bullies do things to you and say things about you because of issues they have with themselves, not issues they have with you. But I also understand that sometimes, as much as you try, those words *can* hurt and those wounds can last.

. . .

NOT A JOKING MATTER

A lot of times, when a parent or teacher tells a kid that they are using words to hurt and/or scare another kid, they try to pass of their remarks as just jokes. "I'm only teasing her," you hear bullies say. But hurtful cracks are some of the cruelest weapons that bullies can use against a helpless kid.

Sure, I understand that everybody jokes around. And there's nothing wrong with having fun with your friends. None of us wants to be too sensitive. There's nothing wrong with being able to take a joke.

But everyone needs to know the difference between "good" teasing and "bad" teasing. There are some very clear ways you can tell the difference between jokes among buddies and harmful insults from bullies.

BUDDIES:
- Joke around in ways that make you both laugh.
- Don't joke to hurt your feelings on purpose.
- Stop joking if they think they might hurt your feelings.
- Don't get angry if you joke back with them.

BULLIES:
- Always use jokes to hurt you.

· Refuse to allow you to joke in return.
· Keep insulting you even after they know they have hurt your feelings.
· Often get upset when you ignore their jokes.

RELATIONSHIP BULLYING

Edward wants badly to hang out with Chris and his group of friends. Chris and his buddies are known as some of the coolest kids in the school. They play sports. The girls all like them. They have all the newest and best video games. They have cool clothes and haircuts.

At first Edward tries really hard to be their friend. He always says hi to Chris in the classes they share and when he sees Chris

22

walking to or from school. He always laughs at Chris's jokes, even when they aren't that funny. And even though Edward's parents don't have a lot of money, Edward is always after them to buy him clothes like Chris and his friends wear. But whenever Edward asks for an expensive pair of designer jeans or sneakers, his mother shakes her head and reminds Edward that she is having a hard enough time making sure their family has all the basics: food, the bills paid, a car to get to school and work. But Edward does whatever he can to try and keep up with Chris and his group of pals.

One day Edward lets Chris steal answers on a test, hoping that Chris might like him if he helps him cheat.

The truth is, nothing Edward tries works. Chris and his buddies will never accept Edward into their group. As a matter of fact, the more Edward tries, the more they seem to not want to hang out with him.

They never invite him into their games. Never ask him to come to any of their parties. Whenever they see Chris at the mall, they won't make eye contact with him. Chris never even acknowledges Edward's attempts to be his friend.

Finally, one day, as Edward is approaching them in gym class, he hears another boy say to Chris, "Uh-oh, here comes the pest, man. I really wish you'd tell this guy to quit coming around. He's so lame." Chris just grins and walks with his friend to the other end of the gym. Edward is really hurt. He's never done anything mean to the guys. In fact, he always goes out of his way to try to be part of their group. But no matter what he does, they turn their backs on him, refusing to speak to him. All they ever do is make fun of him.

At first Edward tries to act like these things don't hurt his feelings. He just walks away, sometimes even pretending that they haven't heard him say hi or that they didn't notice him trying to walk over to hang out with them.

But he knows that isn't really what's happening. He knows that Chris and his friends don't want him in their circle. They don't think he's "cool" enough, and after a while, Edward decides they are right. He never has had the cool clothes or great games. Nobody ever picked him for their sports teams during basketball and football games. Once he starts thinking like this, he starts calling himself the same bad names that Chris's friends use on him, names like "lame" and "loser."

Edward spends so much time beating on himself that he never realizes that maybe Chris and his friends aren't "cool enough" to hang out with him. Instead he grows more and more unhappy with himself. He figures that it's his fault that they turn their backs on him and call him hurtful names.

Relationship bullying happens to you when kids keep you

out of their social groups just to be mean. Or when kids use their social groups to gang up on you and make you feel bad for not being part of their groups. Relationship bullying also takes place when kids force you to do things against your will. They may tell you that you're not "one of them" or "not cool" if you don't do something, usually something dangerous or against the rules—or hurtful to someone else. Sometimes what they want you to do may just be stupid or embarrassing. But sometimes, in relationship bullying, a group of kids may make you try to do something that will get you in trouble with your teachers, your parents, or even the police.

There are many ways that groups can be mean. Sometimes kids who are on sports teams are mean to you if you aren't on a team. Sometimes kids in different clubs or from different neighborhoods attack students who don't come from their area. Other times people get left out of groups because of things like their ethnic or racial background or because of a physical or mental disability.

TYPES OF RELATIONSHIP BULLIES

Relationship bullies come in various types. Here are a few that you should be able to recognize and—with some help—deal with:

25

The Two-Faced Friend: These are bullies who try to act like they are your friends but then use their status to pressure you into doing dumb things. They tell you thing like, "You've got to do this if you want to hang out with us" and "You're not my friend if you don't do this." They try to get you to do things that help them or that hurt others, and they really don't care about your feelings or any consequences you might suffer. For example, some kids may try to convince you to help them cheat on a test, saying stuff like, "I won't be your friend anymore if you don't let me get answers from your worksheet." Or someone may try to get you to tease another kid or steal his things. He or she may tell you that if you don't go along with him or her, they'll hurt you or tease you. And if you get caught doing anything that the Two-Faced Friend says, you can be sure that he or she will be the first person to blame it all on you.

The Stuck-up Kid: These bullies try to act as if they are better than you and usually try to keep you out of their circle of friends. They turn their backs on you or turn up their noses when you come around, bragging about how they have something over you.

26

The Bad Mouth: These bullies usually like to spread rumors about others. They get together with their friends and tell all kinds of stories about you—especially if you are weaker or smaller or less popular than they are. In many cases, they will not say these bad things to your face. They would rather tell other people about you and

see if the rumors get back to you. When those rumors do reach you, Bad Mouths will usually deny saying anything at all. But they will go right back to repeating rumors and lies as soon as they get the chance.

Group Bullies: In many of the incidents we've talked about so far, the harassment doesn't involve a single bully, but rather a group of kids. There are a lot of reasons that some kids help a bully pick on other kids:

- They're scared that the bully will target them instead of you if they don't help the bully.

- They don't want to be seen as "different" from other kids, so they follow along.
- They get the same pleasure out of bullying as the lead bully.

Almost every group is formed by people with something in common; they may come from the same communities or have had similar life experiences. And there's nothing wrong with guys and girls with similar backgrounds getting together to hang out. But when a group turns against just one other person, especially because their background is different, it's not right.

Group bullies use their combined might to give you a hard time. Sometimes the bullies limit their actions to stupid pranks, insults, and other silly behavior. Sometimes these small things can lead to other, worse incidents. Sometimes group bullies will attack you physically. In other cases, group bullies will organize attacks in different ways: online, through whispers, by excluding you from a group activity or a common place where everyone gets together. Group bullies might claim a table in the cafeteria as theirs, threatening to hurt anybody not in their group who tries to sit in that part of the lunchroom.

Group bullies usually stick together in a gang as a way of protecting themselves. Because of this, many kids who are part of bullying groups stop really, truly being themselves. They no longer think about their actions as their own. Instead they think that because they are doing what the rest of the group is doing, they are not responsible for their actions. This mentality has led to some pretty terrible events in the recent past. It is also another good example of bullies picking on someone simply because of the situation that they themselves are in. Always remember that if you are being bullied, it is not because of you. There is nothing wrong with you. You are not asking to be bullied in any way. It is not your fault. You are being bullied because of something that needs to change in the bully, not because of something that needs to change in you. In this particular type of bullying, you may be the target of a group of bullies only because none of the bullies has the courage to say to the others that picking on you is wrong, so they go along with it.

If you are their target, group bullies can be dangerous because of the strength of their numbers. But these groups are also harmful to the kids who are part of them. As I just said, acting as part of a group of bullies can cloud their judgment and make them forget that they are individuals with the power to stand on their own and do the right thing. And again, that is not your fault.

GIRL BULLYING

The stereotypical bully, the one that comes to mind first, is a boy. Whenever we think about kids who are too aggressive or mean or willing to hit other kids, many of us think that is behavior that only boys carry out. But this is just not true. Some of the worst acts of bullying we've seen in recent years have been committed by girls. And we're not just talking about gossiping or excluding people from groups, which can be devastating, but also the sorts of bullying tactics traditionally associated with what many people now call "mean girls."

Now, in many cases, "mean girls" are also getting physical with kids like you. Brutal beatings have been retold on message boards, captured on videotape, and posted on YouTube. It seems that girl bullies are becoming as tough and vicious as the male bullies we're used to.

Many experts say that girls today bully as much as, if not more than, boys. This means you've got to make sure you keep an eye out for everyone around you, because you never know who might be a victim or a bully. Many adults are quicker to react if they think you are being bullied by a boy instead of a girl—they think girls just aren't capable of inflicting the same kind of harm a boy can. This is wrong, of course, and you should never make the mistake of dismissing a bullying act because a girl did it. We will talk later about what you should do if you do see someone being bullied, but right now I just want to talk about what you should pay attention to.

While violence among girl bullies is growing, many girls continue to use social groups as a weapon. Relationship bullying occurs among girls and boys, but girls seem to turn to this tactic more often. Verbal bullying is also a tactic

preferred by girls. While boys can and will insult each other's looks and body types, girls who are bullies turn to these type of put-downs more often. Girl bullies also use the rumor mill as a powerful weapon against people they don't like, and they are quick to spread lies.

While many boy bullies are willing to "get their hands dirty" by directly confronting you, girl bullies often try to get someone else to pick on or attack you. Research has shown that girl bullies like to sit back and watch others do their dirty work. Apparently they get enjoyment and a sense of power from this. Remember, though, that the types of bullying chosen by girls are just as painful as the types preferred by the boys. Just because there are no physical bruises doesn't mean that there are no emotional scars.

Among boys, a bully might be the biggest or strongest kid, though not necessarily the best-known or best-liked student. Among girls, bullies tend to be the popular girls in a school. They often act like bullies to keep other girls out of their circles or away from boys they like. They divide people into "acceptable" and "unacceptable" groups based on things like hairstyles, clothes, shoes, and looks. On the surface, these girls seem to be well liked, but often that isn't true. Instead they are feared.

Of course, the reverse may also be the case: Girls who are left out and overlooked sometimes turn into bullies as a way of getting attention. These girls may not think they are pretty enough or cool enough to hang out with the popular girls. So as a way of dealing with the pain of feeling inferior to others, they start fights, say mean things, and try to hurt others.

Girls who are bullied have to take special care not to let the attacks hurt them over a long period of time. Doesn't it make sense? Girls who are bullied grow up to become women who tolerate bullying in their relationships and in their marriages. Many women who are hurt by their husbands grew up thinking that they had to put up with bullying. It's very important that girls learn early what bullying is and how to stop it.

BASICS OF BULLYING

Even though there are many different types of bullying, they all have some things in common. Here are a few ways you can tell that someone is acting like a bully.

Bullies usually harm those they see as "weaker" or "different." In many cases, bullies are physically bigger. Other times they are considered more popular than other kids and have larger groups of friends. In some cases, the bullies come from a richer family or are part of popular social or athletic groups. But whenever someone tries to bully you or someone you know, it's always because they *think* they can convince you that you're somehow weaker than they are. Remember, though, that just because a bully thinks that you are weaker, different, or not as cool, that does *not* mean that you are!

Bullies do harm on purpose. Bullying isn't a mistake kids make. They don't accidentally hurt your feelings through mean acts that they commit over and over again. Bullying is done on purpose, with the intent to hurt or embarrass you. Sure, there are times when kids joke around with

34

you and sometimes accidentally hurt your feelings or your body. In these cases, an apology is certainly in order, but that one mean act doesn't necessarily amount to you being bullied. Bullying is much more than this. It is intentional, it is hurtful, and it is not okay.

Bullies don't do it just once. If it's just one mean act, then an apology and an agreement not to do or say that hurtful thing again should be enough to fix the problem. But bullying isn't about one single act against you. Bullies usually repeat their behavior. Girls who get pushed around or boys who have rumors spread about them on message boards don't usually suffer just once. The bullies who attack you do it over and over again because they are always looking for ways to put you down—which makes them feel better about themselves. And in many cases, the situation goes from bad to worse for kids like you. Bullies have been known to start with taunting and then move into physical bullying that can grow worse over time. Bullying even once is not okay, and we will talk later about how to stop it before it gets (or once it does get) out of control.

Bullies nearly always play to an audience. Sure, sometimes a bully will corner you in an empty hallway and make threats or actually carry them out. But bullying is usually done for other people to see. Bullies don't just want to prove their power over you. They also want to make sure that other people know that they have—or think they have—some sort of control over how you feel and act, where you can and can't go, who you hang out with, or what games you participate in. Bullying is usually very public. It is important to recognize bullying when you see it. Later in this book I am going to give you a great, proven plan for stopping bullying, but if you don't recognize it, you can never stop it, so remember these points.

CHAPTER SUMMARY

Bullying includes any type of insulting or threatening behavior that is repeated over and over and is aimed at children seen as physically or socially weaker than the bully or different from the bully.

Three major types of bullying are physical bullying, verbal bullying, and relationship bullying.

Physical bullying involves the use or threat of physical violence to humiliate, manipulate, and/or frighten another child.

Verbal bullying involves using spoken words to attack or embarrass another child.

Relationship bullying means that the bully is using his or her social status to hurt another child. This involves keeping kids out of social groups, using a child's desire to belong to a group to force the child to misbehave or do something he/she doesn't want to do, or spreading rumors and insults about other children through friends, neighbors, or schoolmates.

Bullying is always intentional, and unless it's stopped, it usually gets worse as times goes by.

JOURNAL EXERCISES

Writing out your thoughts in journal form is a great way to organize your ideas and feelings and to better express them. Take some time to write down your thoughts about the various forms of bullying we've talked about. Here are few things to ask yourself that might help you get started:

- Has someone else ever physically picked on me? What did I do about it?

- Have I ever bullied someone in any form before?

- What are some of the most hurtful things someone has said about me? Did I think these things were true? If I did, why did I believe these things? If I didn't, how was I able to keep from believing them?

- Have I ever spread rumors about someone else?

- Has anyone ever cyberbullied me? How did I react? What did I do?

- Does anyone try to keep me out of a group or prevent me from joining in a game or activity? Do I do that to anyone else? If so, why? How does it make me feel when I see that someone isn't allowed to play with me or other kids?

2
E-BULLYING

Sandra hadn't spoken to Lynn in weeks. The two had been pretty good friends up until they had gotten into an argument at another friend's house. Someone told Lynn that Sandra was spreading rumors about her. Sandra knew this wasn't true, and told Lynn. But Lynn didn't believe her.

Sandra is hurt that Lynn won't talk to her, but she hopes that Lynn will get over it. But then one evening, Sandra signs on to her MySpace page and reads a bunch of mean messages that Lynn has written about her. She's called Sandra names, made fun of her clothes, and even dissed Sandra's parents and family.

Pretty soon, Lynn is leaving messages about Sandra every few days. She tells mean jokes about Sandra and even gets some of her friends to write bad stuff. She also starts sending nasty text messages to Sandra's cell phone, calling her "liar" and "cow."

Sandra grows more and more frightened by Lynn's behavior. She has known Lynn for a long time, but didn't know she could be so mean. Sandra begins to wonder who else is reading the messages and whether people who don't really know her will believe these things. She begins to stay away from places where Lynn might be, and hangs out less with her friends.

And then Lynn begins posting even meaner things about Sandra on her own site. She and some older boys post ugly drawings of Sandra and spread rumors about her.

Even after Sandra takes her own Web page down, the online attacks continue. Night after night, Sandra goes on to Lynn's website and sees new insults and cruel jokes. There are even some threats, including a few that really intimidate Sandra after she notices how some girls at school were starting to stare at her. And of course the text messages keep getting worse.

Sandra tries to keep quiet about the incidents. She doesn't want to show how the insults hurt her, but the pain becomes too great. After about two months of putting up with the website, and weeks of crying alone in her room, Sandra finally tells her mother about it. Her mom contacts Lynn's parents the next afternoon. Lynn's mom has never paid much attention to her daughter's online activities, but she is bothered right away. She demands that Lynn take her site down and apologize to Sandra. She also demands that the text messages stop. They do.

Lynn and Sandra never become friends again. They stop talking and avoid each other whenever possible. Sandra has a tough time patching things up with some of the other students who joined in. Sandra was accused of some very mean things, and some of the kids believed the lies. It will take a long time for Sandra to get her good name back.

Online bullying (also known as "cyberbullying") is a newer form of bullying than the others we have talked about. Online bullying involves using the Internet to attack, insult, threaten, and spread rumors about other people. As more kids spend more time in chat rooms and on message boards and other places on the Web, some of them take their conflicts with other children online, too. Bullies like to have an audience watching them while they act out. Technology has given them a bigger audience than ever before.

Once children were pushed around mostly on the neighborhood playground or the schoolyard. When it comes to bullying nowadays, though, the Internet has made the playground a whole lot bigger.

FAST FACT

The number of children reporting online harassment has gone up by 50 percent since 2000. *(Source: U.S. Center for Disease Control and Prevention)*

Cyberbullying also makes it easier for children to hide their identities. As a result, online bullies aren't always the biggest or toughest people in the neighborhood or at the school. Sometimes bullies who harass other children online are just kids filled with anger or hatred, who think that the Internet gives them the best way to express their feelings. Of course, online bullying can also just be another outlet for people who are involved in other, more direct forms of bullying. A child who is bullied online often has to deal with other forms of bullying, too. And it's usually from the same person or group of children involved in the online conflict.

Cyberbullying can take a lot of different forms. In Sandra's case, there were two clear examples of cyberbullying. First, Lynn and others left nasty messages about her on personal websites. More and more kids are creating websites that involve some form of attacks on other children: sites that "rate" other children, sites where people post hurtful messages and images, and sites that give personal information about others that can be used to embarrass them.

Second, Lynn sent Sandra mean text messages. Cyber-bullying doesn't just begin or end with PCs or Macs. Cyberbullying can also involve mean messages or photos sent over cell phones. Children have reported having their number bombed with message after message filled with terrible insults from other people. Text-message bully-ing is a distant relative to old-fashioned phone bullying, where people would call up different homes and make crank remarks, shout insults, or just hang up and call back over and over.

Some other forms of Internet bullying include:

E-mailing mean pictures: Nowadays, cell phones can take videos and still photos. As a result, bullies use these devices to embarrass other children. People have talked about bullies taking bad pictures of them with cell phones and e-mailing them to other people. There have also been cases where bullies have e-mailed pictures that they claimed were of their victims but really weren't.

Stealing someone's online ID:

Another way bullies can hurt people online is by pretending to be them in chat rooms and on message boards. Children may imitate another child's sign-on name and then show up in a popular room where that person may hang out online. They will then start to say mean or embarrassing things about the child, pretending it's the victim saying these things about himself. Or the bully may make it seem as though the person he/she is pretending to be is saying something bad about other people. Many conflicts have been started because someone went online and pretended to be speaking as someone else. This is one of the sneakiest and most hurtful forms of cyberbullying, because it makes it harder for you to know who is behind this act.

Stealing passwords: In some cases, someone can get hold of your password and make your life miserable. Sometimes they will use the password to sign on as you and make trouble with your friends or even strangers. In other cases, bullies use the stolen password to sign you up to receive junk mail from different websites, including places where dangerous strangers may hang out. Or the bullies might even give your password to others, who can use it to hack into your system and even steal your private information.

Stolen passwords can lead to more than insults and rumors being posted online. Bullies have given stolen passwords to criminals who use them to break into bank accounts and use credit cards. They can steal a lot of money this way. Stolen passwords have contributed to crimes not only against kids, but also against their parents. This can lead to trouble far beyond what a child bully may cause for a classmate or neighbor.

Keeping children out of online games: Interactive games have been popular for years, and they have become a way for bullies to pick on others. Children have discussed how they are sometimes not allowed into certain game rooms or onto certain teams during games because bullies keep them away. In the same way that smaller children are sometimes not allowed to join in basketball or football games, online bullies can keep less popular people out of online social groups during gaming activities.

Staging fights to post on YouTube: In many cases, online bullying can be a sign that a child is being picked on physically, too. There have been recent reports of incidents

where kids have attacked other kids and taped the fights to post online later. These attacks have led to some horrifying footage, showing girls and boys being kicked, punched, and shoved, and having their hair pulled and their bodies bruised. Although this constitutes physical bullying, the bully adds to the humiliation of his or her victim by broadcasting the mean acts for all to see. In one well-known case, some girls beat up another girl from their school and shot video of the attack while some guys acted as lookouts for them. The video was then posted on YouTube for everyone to see. Eventually, seven teen bullies were arrested for the attack and charged with battery and false imprisonment.

Sending viruses: Some kids intentionally send out code that is meant to damage a victim's computer or software. There are also viruses that let the bullies spy on what other kids are doing or even take control of their computers.

CHAPTER SUMMARY

Online bullying involves the use of computers, websites, message boards, and other online forums to hurt other kids.

Cyberbullying is another name for online bullying.

The Internet now gives bullies a bigger audience.

Online bullying can sometimes indicate that physical bullying is also going on.

Online bullying can involve forms of verbal bullying when kids leave nasty messages or texts on others' phones or computers or Web pages.

Online bullying can also provide a place for relationship bullying as some kids sometimes keep others out of online games and other activities.

Bullies sometimes steal people's online identities and send embarrassing or threatening messages to others.

Online bullying can lead to financial and other crimes.

3
WHY DO KIDS BULLY OTHERS?

Jake walks into school every day with a big smile. The big seventh-grade boy strolls confidently to his locker, takes off his jacket, and just stands around waiting for the younger, smaller kids to start walking by. When they do, he picks a kid at random, sticks his foot out, and tries to trip the kid, laughing really loudly whenever a kid walks over his outstretched leg and falls down.

Many days go like that for Jake. But the evenings aren't nearly as fun for the bully. That's when Jake gets home and finds his older brother, Tommy, waiting for him. Every day

Tommy grabs Jake in a headlock or pulls his ears. "What's happenin', kiddo?" he asks.

Tommy bullies Jake in other ways too. He often takes food out of his hands while Jake is eating it. He shoves Jake out of the way to get to the fridge. He calls Jake mean names whenever he gets mad at his younger brother.

Jake complains to his parents, but they see Tommy's actions as harmless fun. "Don't be such a wimp," Jake's dad says. "Don't tattle so much," his mother scolds.

So Jake just tries to take Tommy's bullying in stride. He knows his older brother loves him, but he can't stand the way the bullying makes him feel. He needs ways to feel better about himself.

And that's where the smaller kids at school come in. Jake bullies them because he figures that since Tommy picks on him, he can do the same thing to his schoolmates. But the truth is, picking on the smaller kids doesn't make Jake feel much different about himself on the inside. He still feels bad about how Tommy treats him.

There are a lot of reasons that bullies pick on other children. Even before we get to some of the causes behind bullying, I think it's important that everyone accepts one true fact about bullying: It's never the victim's fault. That means, if you are getting bullied, it is NOT YOUR FAULT! And furthermore, it has nothing to do with you. Bullies do the things they do because of them, not because of you. Please know that if you are being bullied right now, it doesn't mean that there is something wrong with you, and if bullies call you names, do not believe them.

There are many things that create bullying, but it is NEVER, EVER because the kid who gets picked on deserves to be treated badly. No one deserves to be bullied. And one of the worst mistakes a bully's victim can make is to believe that they somehow have brought the bullying on themselves.

Just because somebody picks on you doesn't make you uncool or stupid or weird—but it does put you in the spotlight. Bullies call you out, put attention on you that you don't want. They mistreat you in front of everyone: your buddies, that girl you may have a crush on, the younger kids at school. And in doing this, bullies try to destroy your self-esteem—how you feel about yourself.

That doesn't mean you have to change who you are. Be yourself. Love yourself. You shouldn't feel like you have to be just like everyone else. It's okay to like your music, your books, your movies, and your TV programs. You don't have to look down on other people's likes, and you don't have to go along with their dislikes. You want to treat people kindly, and you should ask that people do the same to you. Bullying, of course, goes against these ideas in every way.

KNOW YOUR VALUE

Later on in this book I'll talk a whole lot more about what victims of bullying can do, so I won't go into all the ways that you can deal with bullies here. But I do want to talk about your responsibility to you, not as someone being bullied or as a bully, even—your responsibility to yourself as a good person. You are a great person. You're someone who is likeable and who can be a winner, no matter what someone else may say. You have to believe this. You have to believe in yourself and your importance—because believing in yourself will set you on the path to being a winner. Bullies try to make you feel as if you're small and unimport- ant. But that's not true— and overcoming bullies first means that you start to really believe in your heart that what they are saying about you isn't true.

Yes, there are any number of steps you can take to prevent bullying, but before you can take them, you need to accept that the power to take them is yours. You're not to blame for bullying, but you have to be the one who stops the bullying in your life. You don't have to do it alone, but you can and must stop it.

One of the first things that you have to be careful of is that you don't bully yourself. You bully yourself when you believe the lies that a bully says about you and then call yourself the names that they call you. You're not a dork. You're not stupid or lame. You're smart. You're capable. You're a worthwhile person. But if you accept the bully's taunts, you're only adding to the abuse that you're taking from him or her.

I've talked to older students about this subject before, and I'll discuss it more later in this book. But I just want to let you know that you have to view yourself as a good person before you can expect other kids to see you the same way. You can affect how other people treat you by the way you act. So no, it's not a guy or girl's fault if a bully taunts him or her. But the victims are also the people who have the most power to step up and handle the situation. Don't think of bullying as your fault, ever. But always know that you have the ability, and the responsibility, to bring it to an end in your life. And when you grab hold of this power and make it yours, you can stop bullies from hurting you.

WHAT MAKES A BULLY?

So that brings us to this question: If you can't blame the victim, who—or what—do you blame?

Well, people who study the way kids behave have a lot of ideas about what makes some children want to pick on others. All of them agree that bullying is about the negative emotions inside bullies.

Bullies have certain attitudes that contribute to how they behave. Here are some of the attitudes that can shape a bully's behavior:

They get a kick out of taking advantage of you. Not all bullies are bad people, of course, but there are bullies who do enjoy hurting you if they think of you as weaker or different.

They think they have the right to bully you. Bullies need to think of themselves as "special," as better than you. And this thinking also leads them to believe that because they are special, they can treat you badly.

Bullies are blind to your feelings; they either can't or don't like to see things from your point of view. They think that the only real way of looking at things is their way. They can't imagine that you might actually have a different outlook from them, and if you do, then you're just plain wrong and a problem for them.

They have a hard time accepting that you are different in some way. Bullies think you should act like them or think like them or look like them. They want you to enjoy the movies and clothes and toys they do and look at everyone the same way.

They take out their anger or sadness on you. Bullies like to blame you for how they feel inside. Because bullies often have a hard time dealing with their own feelings, it's sometimes easier for them to use you as a way of showing their frustration, anger, or sadness.

They have a hard time seeing how their behavior might affect things over time. Bullies don't always think about what could happen to them or to you if they keep up the bullying. They can't understand why anyone would— or should—try to stop them from harming you. This is important, because you should know that oftentimes a bully doesn't know or even think about how hard it is for you to deal with their actions. Being a bully is often fun for them, and that's all they think about. Hopefully, a lot of bullies would stop what they were doing if they knew how truly mean it was.

They want attention. Bullies think they look cool when they pick on you. They think it makes them tough or funny. Once again, many bullies don't feel good about themselves. So they think that by picking on you, they will get attention that will make them feel better about who they are.

BULLIES DO IT BECAUSE THEY CAN

I said earlier that there are no innocent bystanders, and we will talk more about that later. But that doesn't mean that people don't overlook acts of bullying every day. And that is another reason bullies get the courage to continue picking on a neighbor or a classmate. They do it because people, including the kids being bullied, let them get away with it. When you don't stand up and try to stop a bully, the bully only gets worse over time.

Look, I get that a lot of kids, your friends maybe, don't stand up to bullies because they think that as long as the bully's not picking on them, everything's cool. It doesn't make you a bad person if you don't intervene between a bully and his or her victim—in fact, by stepping in directly, you might put yourself at risk. Also, many kids are more concerned about how they look to their friends than about doing what's right. So if you see other people ignoring a bully's behavior, you might feel like there's nothing wrong with you letting it slide too. Meanwhile, other kids are just trying to keep a handle on their own problems and may feel they've got enough trouble to deal with without taking on someone else's issues too.

But you do owe it to yourself and others around you to speak out when you know someone is being hurt. And when you don't, you aren't just avoiding the problem. You're adding to it. Even if you aren't joining in with the bully to pick on another kid, your refusal to do anything about it makes you *just as bad as the bully.*

I've talked to kids all over the country about this, because I think it's very important for young people to understand that, as a group, we have the power to stop bullying. I'm going to spend most of this book talking about what individuals can to do protect themselves against bullying, but I've got to say that there is still no power like the kind that comes from being with a group of people who are doing the right thing. And bullies are only really effective when they don't have anyone willing to call them out on their bad behavior and stand up to them.

THE MAKING OF A BULLY

No one wakes up one day and just says, "You know, I think I'm going to start bullying my neighbors today." Bullies aren't born to pick on other kids, although some scientists do think there may be a genetic component to what makes one person want to hurt another. And bullies don't just fall out of the sky, either. But they do come from somewhere. I'm sad to say that the most common place where bullies are made is right there in the comfort—or discomfort—of their own homes.

I know that most parents don't want to think they might be raising a bully, the same way most bullies don't really see themselves as kids who pick on weaker kids. They would rather see themselves as the "cool" kid or

the "popular" guy or girl who just happens to tell it like it is, even if that means making someone else feel bad. They don't see anything wrong with the way they mistreat someone. And in the same way, some parents have a hard time understanding that, even though they don't mean to, they may very well be one of the biggest contributors to the making of a bully.

Home life is at the root of almost all kinds of bullying that kids have to endure. Many times young bullies treat other people the way they are treated, or the way they see their parents, older brothers and sisters, or other family members treat others. They also learn how to treat others based on the types of rules that parents set for them and the different ways that those rules are enforced. In some cases, the parents were bullies—or still are—and have passed certain types of behavior along. In other cases, the parents may have been the victims of bullies and never learned to deal with the issue of bullying properly. As a result, they were never able to teach their kids the lessons necessary to keep them from attacking or hurting others.

In still other cases, parents try to teach the right lessons but aren't always attentive to how their kids treat one another. As a result, older siblings sometimes push their younger sisters or brothers around. Parents may see this as a harmless form of fun or sibling rivalry. The truth is, it can leave the younger or smaller kids feeling isolated and unprotected. This may make them easier for other kids to bully, or it may make them bullies outside of the home, feeling like it's now their turn to have the "fun" of bullying another person.

PARENTS CAN ENCOURAGE BULLYING

You may not realize it, and your parents may not realize it, but lots of kids learn how to be a bully from adults. Grown-ups should never bully their children or other grown-ups.

The problem is, usually parents do not even know that they are being a bully toward their kid. But there are ways you can tell. According to Barbara Coloroso, author of a book called *The Bully, the Bullied and the Bystander*, bully parents are those who:

· Try to have absolute control over their kids. They tell their children to do what they say "because

I said so." This makes kids want to go and boss around or control someone else.

· Threaten their children with spankings or other violence. This teaches children to use violence to control other people or to be afraid when they are threatened.

· Attempt to humiliate or embarrass their children as a way to punish them. Bullies often learn how to make fun of others from parents who tease them.

· Rule by fear. This is dangerous because it may cause a child to be weak and passive—or scary and aggressive—when someone threatens them. And if they don't get what they want, they may bully others to get it. These kids don't do the right thing because it is the right thing to do; they do what they want to get what they want.

· Push competition and contests too much. A child may learn that winners are better and anyone who doesn't win is a loser. This also teaches kids that they have to beat—or beat up—other kids in order to be important.

· Teach their kids that mistakes are bad. When these kids make mistakes, they may start to think that they are no good—and really start to act that way.

- Tell their kids what to say, what to do, and what to think. They don't teach their kids how to think through or solve problems. If kids do not learn how to solve problems or think for themselves, they will do whatever other people tell them to do. That is a very dangerous thing.

KNOW YOUR BULLY

If you're the person being picked on by a bully, you probably don't want to hear me say this, but I feel like it's something that needs to be pointed out: Kids who bully others aren't necessarily bad people. In fact, in some areas of their lives, bullies may seem to be doing a pretty good job—at

least on the outside. They may be good teammates on a sports squad or loyal friends to folks in their circles. Bullies may be helpful to their parents at home and supportive of brothers and sisters.

Bullies are potentially good people, but they are doing a very bad thing in hurting other children. As we've pointed out, bullies often overlook the fact that their victims are people who deserve to be treated the same way anyone else is. Or they have a tough time handling their emotions, so they take out anger or frustration or fear on kids they think will put up with the abuse. But whatever the case, they are intruding on someone else's right to grow up without being abused. And it's this fact that makes other people see them and label them as bullies.

You should always ask yourself what a bully is getting out of a situation. Why is he doing what he's doing? Here are some questions you should ask yourself when trying to understand why a bully is picking on you:

· What's he getting out of it? Power? Joy? Revenge?
· Is there something about your personality that
  pushes the bully's buttons? (I'm not saying you
  have to change anything about yourself here,
  but you should be aware of it if it's part of the
  problem.)
· Is the bully sad or hurting on the inside? Can you
  tell? Are there ways, without putting yourself at
  risk or looking like you are desperate to be his or
  her friend, that you can help the bully?

- Is bullying "just the way things are" at your school? Do the older kids pick on the younger kids? Do the bigger kids go after the smaller kids?
- Does the bully really like you or envy you—but just doesn't know how to say so in the right way?
- Was the bully trained to be a bully? Does he have a bullying parent? Can you understand why he or she does it?

One big step in taking on bullies is understanding why they behave the way they do. So look them in the eye and pay close attention. After a while, you'll begin to understand why they do what they do.

I'm not saying you have to put up with bullying, but you should try to realize that the bully is also a person with his or her own sets of feelings, ideas, and values. He or she may think that bullying gets a person "respect," whether kids like the bully or not. But of course, what bullies really want is to be liked; they just don't know how to come out and say so. Sometimes a friendly gesture or a kind word may be part of what it takes to help turn a bully around.

It may not always be that easy. I don't want y'all to think that there's some magical word you can say or that you can always talk to a bully and end a conflict there. And you don't want to be kind to a bully only to create an opening for the bully to hurt you later.

But as tough as it may be, it never hurts to recognize that even people who bother or hurt you are still people themselves. And sometimes what they are really looking for is someone to tell them that they don't have to behave a certain way to be friends, that they could be liked for who they are if only they'd give it a try. Like all of us, bullies often want someone to recognize that they are people with needs and wants too. They just never learned how to ask for that kind of positive attention.

Of course, there are those people who have been so screwed up by things that have happened to them in the past that you're probably not going to reach them with the usual attempts at friendship. Frankly, there are some bullies out there who are downright frightening, kids and gangs of kids who will do almost anything to torment other children. Kids, parents, and teachers have to be mindful that when these kids bully others, their actions can lead to some potentially life-threatening situations.

If you are dealing with that kind of bully, you need to

avoid him or her. Seriously. Run the other way when you see that person coming. Go immediately to a teacher or another adult in charge if that bully begins to bother you. Don't fight, because you might get hurt yourself. Just get away as fast as you can. There is nothing wrong with avoiding a fight; it does not make you a weak person, and telling a teacher or parent is not tattling! Telling an adult is responsible and necessary. So don't ever hesitate to do either.

CHAPTER SUMMARY

You count, you're important, and you don't ever deserve to be bullied.

Bullies have certain traits:

- They take advantage of other kids.
- They think they have the right to bully.
- They don't like to see other people's points of view.
- They won't accept that everyone is different.
- They take out their anger or sadness on others.
- They don't think ahead when they bully.
- They want attention.

Bullies get away with picking on kids when other kids let them.

Bullies have learned to be bullies from someone else or some situation in their lives.

Bullies are often bullied themselves by someone older.

Bullies can learn negative traits from parents and older siblings.

While some bullies really are bad people, most bullies are potentially good people doing bad things.

Parents have to be careful to teach the right behavior to kids.

JOURNAL EXERCISES

- What are some of the ways that I have bullied myself? Have I ever believed that insults about me were really true? Have I ever said these things about myself?

- What are some of the negative attitudes I see in bullies around me? Do I have any of these negative attitudes myself? Where do these attitudes come from?

- Have I seen parents do things that I think might lead to bully behavior in kids? What are some of the things they have done that might help turn their kid into a bully?

- Have I ever watched someone get bullied and ignored it? Why didn't I take action? How did that make me feel?

- Have I ever tried to stop a bully from picking on someone else? How did I do it and why? Did I feel better for taking action?

4

THE DAMAGE
BULLIES CAN DO

Still with me, right? Don't stop reading now! What we're about to discuss is some serious and important stuff. You need to know what damage bullying can do over the long term if you hope to change things for the better. As I've said before, people often try to downplay the effects that bullying can have on a kid. But you know same as I do that bullying can hurt you for a long, long time. And sometimes people never really get over being pushed around.

So be aware of what you're dealing with, because it's going to take a real effort from you to turn around a bullying situation. But of course, you know you can do it, right? You have what it takes. But in order for you to solve the problem, you've got to know what it is and what damage it can do if you don't watch out.

As we've discussed, bullying can have far worse affects than bruised feelings or a scraped elbow. Bullying includes beatings, death threats, and harassment. One of the biggest problems with bullying is that too many people think it's no big deal. They say it's just part of growing up. They call it "teasing" or they say kids are only "playing with you." A group of scientists and doctors found out that a whopping 1.6 million kids say they are bullied each year, and 1.7 million are bullying other kids. That's a really big deal.

But usually grownups don't do anything about it until it's too late. That's no good, because bullying brings out the worst in people. There have been lots of news stories over the past few years about violence that has happened to bullies, victims, and bystanders. Deaths in Colorado in 1999 and in California in 2001, along with a lot of other violence from bullying, have led many adults and students to try to put a stop to it. Doctors have figured out that bullying starts in elementary school and is the worst in middle school—and that's why I wrote this book for you. We have to do everything we can to stop this kind of behavior, because bullying can ruin the lives of everyone involved—the kids being bullied, the families (of both the bully and those being bullied), and even the bullies themselves.

BULLYING CAN HURT YOUR BODY IN WAYS YOU DON'T EXPECT

Nobody wants to be hit or beat up. Scars or bruises are sometimes the leftovers from being bullied. These may never go away or could take years to heal, as in the case of

Si'Mone, a boy living in Florida. When he was twelve, Si'Mone was beaten by seven boys on a school bus. One boy was fifteen. A local news station showed the videotape on TV. It was clear that Si'Mone did nothing to start the beating. For months afterward, Si'Mone still had double vision and had a hard time remembering things that had just happened.

Scars are not the only ways that bullying can hurt your body. Fear can also hurt your body. Tyler learned this the hard way:

Last year in the fourth grade, a bunch of boys used to mess with me on the bus. It seemed like they only did it when the bus driver

wasn't looking. Mark would punch me while Brandon and Jamil would stand so that the bus driver couldn't see it. I think they did it because I have a limp. One leg is a little shorter than the other. One day when I saw Mark coming down the aisle in the bus, my head started to feel funny. I felt dizzy. The next thing I remember, the bus driver was fanning me in the face with my math folder. Everybody was scared, including Mark, because they thought that I had a seizure, but really I only fainted.

—Tyler, age nine

Really bad fear stops oxygen from getting to the brain and can make you feel like you are going to faint. When fear gets that bad, it can also cause panic attacks. Maybe you've noticed this feeling in yourself—or have seen it in someone else. A panic attack happens when all of a sudden, you feel so afraid that you feel sick and out of control. Sometimes it comes out of nowhere. It can even happen while a person is sleeping. Most people who have panic attacks say they had the first one when they were a kid. If you experience a few or more of the following at one time, you may be having a panic attack:

· Your heartbeat is really fast.
· It's hard to breathe or move.

- You get dizzy or feel like you have to throw up.
- You start to shake.
- You get diarrhea.
- You feel like you're choking or having chest pains.
- Your body starts to sweat even if you're not hot, or you get chills even if it's not cold.
- Your fingers or toes tingle like you're being poked lightly with tiny pins or needles.

If you think you are having a panic attack, try to breathe slowly and from your belly instead of from your chest. Practice this if you need to: Lie on your back. Put one hand on your chest and the other one on your stomach, between your belly button and your ribs. Focus on letting your stomach go up when you inhale and fall when you breathe out. Hold your chest still. The goal is to breathe easily with your stomach, not your chest, in through your nose and out through your mouth. Even if a panic attack happens only once, talk to your parents, because you may need to see a doctor. Panic attacks might run in your family. Girls especially need to be on the lookout for panic attacks because they happen to girls more often than boys. Doctors do not know why.

You should also watch for other signs of stress, even when

the bully is not around you. If you are jumpy, nervous, irritable, or easily angered, these may be signs that your body is reacting negatively to a bullying situation.

Not only can stress hurt your body directly, but it can lead to you hurting yourself by trying to handle it in the wrong way. For instance, some kids turn to smoking cigarettes, drinking, or doing drugs as a way to deal with the stress of being bullied. Other kids withdraw from their families and friends and become outcasts and loners. Some kids cut themselves out of desperation to relieve stress. In extreme cases, kids feel that they can't cope at all with being bullied and take their own lives.

BULLYING HURTS YOUR MIND

Bullying happens to kids and grown-ups. Even when it is over, the pain you feel in your mind and spirit from being bullied can haunt a victim for years. When people are bullied or teased, they don't always remember what the bully said, but they do remember how the bullying made them feel. Some adults still can remember the times they were bullied and how the experience hurt them. Those feelings can last forever if you don't do something to heal yourself.

Bullying makes the victim feel:

- Afraid. Fear can stop them from trying to reach their dreams.
- Like a loser with low self-esteem.
- Defenseless, like there's nothing they can do to protect themselves.
- Angry, which can cause them to do dumb stuff. It can hurt you too, as I explained earlier. As an ancient wise man called the Buddha once said, "You will not be punished *for* your anger, you will be punished *by* your anger."
- Depressed, feeling down or sad all the time.
- Stressed about being around other people. This is called "social anxiety," and it can keep you from making new friends. It can turn into what's called a phobia. People with phobias imagine that people, things, or places are dangerous even when they are not. It makes you focus on the worst situations instead of the best. Children who have this problem are unsure of themselves, so they try to do whatever the crowd is doing and try to be perfect. They want to please everyone. This leads to the really bad fear of being embarrassed, speaking in front of people, or even eating or drinking in front of people.

· Violent, wanting to hurt the bully or the people who did nothing to stop the bully. Kids who are bullied can feel so hurt and so scared that they always, always think about ways to take revenge. Revenge is never a good idea, because it might involve violence or injuring someone, and it always backfires.

BULLIES BREAK RULES, AND SO DO THEIR TARGETS

Kids' most important job is to do well in school. And believe it or not, there are bullies who do quite well in school. There are also many bullied kids who manage to get As in spite of being pushed around or teased all the time.

But the truth is, bullies and victims often have problems with their schoolwork. Some bullies skip school or drop out. As they get older, bullies are more likely to drink alcohol and take drugs than other kids. And there are victims who are so scared of bullies that they also skip classes or whole days of school. Up to 160,000 students stay home from school each day to avoid a bully. Besides bumps and bruises, flunking (or getting bad grades) is the biggest clue that a kid is getting bullied.

Whenever a kid is a bully, or even a bystander who watches bullying, he or she is breaking rules. Most schools and families have very strict rules against bullying. In order to get away with bullying, a kid may end up not only hurting someone, but also lying to cover it up. That's called "denial." So when you bully someone and then deny it, you've just broken two rules: the rule against bullying and the rule against lying.

There are ways that you can stop this cycle of rule breaking. A person who is bullied has to figure out why the bully is acting mean toward him or her. That's a big step on the path to solving your bully problem. I think bullies break rules because they get something out of it: a payoff. Usually the payoff that the bullies are looking for is power; they want to feel important. Even the kids who are bullied (and break the lying rule in the process) get a payoff. Their payoff is getting the bully to leave them alone—but they've broken a rule, something they might not ordinarily do.

LAWBREAKERS

Bullies have been linked to crimes such as shoplifting and vandalism, as well as more violent crimes, like shootings. By the time they are twenty-four years old, four out of ten adults who used to be bullies will commit at least three crimes.

Bullies who break the law can face consequences that will affect them for the rest of their lives. (Some will go to jail.

Others will be hurt physically. All of them will carry certain emotional scars.) Kids who are bullied sometimes have to deal with lifelong emotional problems too. Bad feelings from being bullied can stay with victims all their lives and cause them to have problems with the law too. Most often the leftover feelings are fear and anger.

BULLYING CAN KILL

It doesn't happen all the time, but enough children have died due to bullying that everyone—including teachers, the Anti-Defamation League, and the president of the United States—is trying to stop it. People who don't know how to deal with the pain of bullying can end up doing something really bad. No matter how nasty bullies can be, typically they don't kill anyone. Bullies look for control over their victim—if they killed the person they are bullying, there would be no one to control. Often it's the victims who can strike back in the worst way. Rarely, but too often, they kill themselves. It's called "bullycide" when a person who is bullied kills himself or herself to escape the bully.

Of course, this is never something you should consider. NO BULLYING IS WORTH TAKING YOUR OWN LIFE! And if you do ever find yourself feeling like the bullying has made life too hard, please go to a teacher, a guidance counselor, a responsible adult—someone—and share how you're feeling, then ask for help. There is always someone who can help, no matter how bad it feels.

JOURNAL EXERCISES

- How does being bullied make my body feel? How do I try to control the physical effects that bullying can have?

- Have I ever felt "social anxiety"? When and where did it happen? Did a bully have anything to do with the feeling? How did I handle the anxiety?

- How do I cope with the stress of being bullied? Do my ways of handling stress help me or hurt me in the long run?

- What are ways that I break rules by bullying someone or by being bullied? Why are these rules important? Why should I try to obey them?

- When I'm with a group of my friends, do I think for myself or just go along with whatever they want to do? If my friends wanted to bully another kid, would I join in or watch?

  - How would I let my friends know that they were doing something I thought was wrong?

5

ARE YOU BEING BULLIED?

Now, as we talked about before, some of you probably don't see yourselves as anything like any of the children mentioned in this book. Maybe you think some of the examples here don't really describe how you get along with your classmates or with the children in your neighborhood. You're not a victim for any bully, right?

Well, I'm not going to say for sure that you're being bullied by anybody right now. Hopefully you aren't and won't ever be. But let's just take a close look at how you're treated by some of the other people around you.

Are there people who make you feel that you can't be yourself around them, and that you need to hide your feelings or ideas just to hang out with them? Do you have friends you follow along with even when you may not want to so that you won't have to worry about them freezing you out of their group? If so, you might be being bullied.

Are there people who make you nervous when they come around because you're afraid they may pick on you? Maybe they've never done anything to you that you can recall, but they've made it clear that crossing them somehow is an unsafe idea. That is the sort of silent intimidation that can lead up to bullying.

Bullying doesn't have to begin with a really hurtful action against you. Sometimes others test you. They take verbal jabs at you just to see how you'll respond. They look to see how you carry yourself and who your friends are or aren't. They size you up. And if they think they can take advantage of you, bullies will strike.

Many times bullies try to act at first as if they're just joking around. They bump into you "by accident"—a lot. They push. They insult. They "borrow" and don't return. But this sort of behavior isn't done in jest, especially not if you don't welcome it. It is part of the early stages of bullying.

Or maybe it's a "class clown" type who is always making a

crack about your clothes, your weight, your height, your hair color, your skin color, your religion, your country of origin, your parents' country of origin, or anything else about you that he or she sees as "different." Sure, at first it seems like it's "just joking around." But maybe it hurts deeper than you want anyone to know. And so you just hide the pain.

Maybe it only happens once. But maybe it happens a second time. And then a third. Are you being bullied? You sure are.

Bullying is really just any type of intimidation of one person by another. Bullies don't have to threaten you with force. Maybe they can't—maybe you're even bigger and stronger. But maybe the bully is more popular and is using that popularity to leave you out of activities or social groups. If so, you're being bullied.

You have the power to end bullying. But the first step toward taking control of the situation is to first acknowledge that it's happening. There's no shame in having it happen to you. It happens to kids all over this country, far too much. You're not alone. And you don't deserve to be mistreated. But you are being bullied, and in order to make it stop, you have to be willing to own up to it.

So how do you know for sure that you're being bullied? Well, a bully's actions are pretty hard to miss—unless you're trying to make excuses for why a kid picks on someone else. So if you find yourself being treated in any of the ways that we've mentioned in chapter one—being verbally or physically abused by someone, being hurt by being left out of social groups and gatherings, or being attacked online—you can be pretty certain that you're being bullied.

But being bullied is not just about what someone else does; it's also about how that person's actions make you feel. And just as you can often identify a bully by his or her behavior, you can also figure out whether you're being bullied by how you feel and behave, too. Here are a few ways you can tell whether you're being bullied in school, at home, or in your neighborhood:

1. You repeatedly make up excuses not to go to school, and often feel sad, angry, frightened, or depressed whenever you are there.

Sure, almost every child has to take a sick day now and then. But if you find that you're constantly trying to come up with a reason to ditch school, you should ask yourself whether there's someone there you're especially trying to avoid. Victims of bullying often stop going to classes because they get sick and tired of being picked on. If showing up at school or the playground makes you want to run and hide because you worry about another student, then you need to address this. It's natural to be a little nervous in some situations, like on your first day in a new class or at a new school. But when it's someone's behavior that's making you feel bad over and over again, you're probably being bullied.

2. You're always being hurt by a particular person or group of people.

Most of us don't want to go through life pushing around other people. But bullies tend to be this way. They are always looking for their victims and seeking out new ways to make some poor kid's life miserable. Bullying isn't just about random conflicts or occasional differences with another person. When you're being bullied, the attacks are constant and usually coming from the same source.

3. You're always being picked on in the presence of other people.

Bullies like to single out others to embarrass them in public. Bullying can happen behind closed doors too, but in many cases, it's all about hurting someone else in front of the largest audience possible. Bullies like an audience, and they usually like to be as loud and showy as possible, too. This is why online bullying is so dangerous, and at the same time, becoming more common: It gives bullies a much bigger place to act out.

4. Someone always turns your mistakes into big deals.

We all make errors. When you make mistakes around bullies, though, they often don't let you forget it. Do poorly on a math test or in gym class, and chances are that a bully will try to make sure you can't live it down.

5. Your belongings are often stolen or taken from you.

The stereotype of the bully who takes another child's lunch money isn't always far from the truth. A bully often tries to make you feel like whatever you own really belongs to him or her. Bullies do things like take a person's jacket and make him "try to get it back" by pleading or jumping up to snatch it from the bully's grasp. They often damage victims' lockers or books or clothing. If you're enduring any of this, you're being bullied.

6. You're always being confronted with lies and rumors.

Verbal bullying is at least as common as physical bullying.

Bullies will often tell other people embarrassing things about you as a way of making you look bad. Bullies use these lies and rumors to get other people to dislike you. Verbal bullying is about singling you out and making you feel like you're "different" and unacceptable to other people. It doesn't matter whether the bully is telling a lie or the truth, because the words are designed for one purpose—to make you hurt.

6

ARE YOU A BULLY?

At the beginning of this book, I told you that I wrote it for anybody out there who is being bullied. But in this chapter I'd like to talk to you about whether *you* might be a bully. Sure, it's possible for you to be a bully and to be the target of a bully at the same time. But as the victim, you have to try and stop someone else from doing something mean to you. If you are the bully, then the only person you need to appeal to is yourself.

You need to realize that bullying is a terrible thing to do to another kid. You don't have the right to make someone else live in fear or embarrassment just because you don't like him or her. When you hurt someone else over and over, you may think you are putting him or her down—but the truth is, you're also damaging yourself. You are showing how petty, mean, silly, and stupid you can be. When you bully someone, you lose sight of his or her rights as a person. In doing so, you can also lose sight of your own character.

If you're a bully, you need to change. You need to figure out just what it is you think you are getting from mistreating other kids, and you need to figure out how to substitute that payoff for something more positive. Remember, though, that while bullying is always unacceptable and what you are doing is 100 percent wrong, that doesn't mean you are a bad person; it just means that you are doing bad things.

Are you letting off steam? Well, if you need to keep picking on someone else, obviously you aren't really getting rid of the source of your anger, are you? You're just hiding from it. Picking on someone isn't going to change whatever it is that is making you angry or sad or frustrated. If you really want to change the source of your emotional pain, you have to confront the source itself, not some poor kid half your size or less popular than you.

Are you trying to prove your superiority? Well, you need to know you're not better than anyone—no matter how much you tease them or shove them down. In fact, when you go out of your way to pick on another kid who can't or won't fight back, you're really just showing other people that you're insecure and emotionally or mentally weak. Think about it: A top athlete like Kobe Bryant doesn't have to go around insulting other players in the NBA. If he's really a better player, his game will do the talking.

Let this same thinking apply to you. If you want to be proud of your accomplishments, that's fine. If you're proud that you have a large circle of friends or great taste in clothes or good grades, you aren't doing anything wrong. But let those accomplishments speak for you. When you bother putting someone else down, you're only showing that you don't think your achievements can stand on their own.

Are you bullying because someone is doing it to you? As I said before, you can't get rid of a problem by harassing someone who isn't part of that problem. If your older brother or some kids on your block are picking on you, then you need to take steps to stop them. Showing up at school and punching on a smaller kid only makes you look cowardly, not suddenly powerful. Plus, you already know what it means to be bullied. You don't like it and wish it'd stop. Why can't you imagine that another kid might think the same thing?

me?

Sure, you might try to tell yourself that you're just joking around or that the kid can take it. But the fact is, you're acting in ways that hurt, scare, or humiliate someone else. You're bullying that kid, plain and simple.

So are you a bully? Well, here are a few ways that experts say they can spot bullies or potential bullies in a crowd:

- You talk or think a lot about violence or have a real interest in violent TV, movies, games, writings, and stories.
- You talk or think about bringing a weapon to school or making weapons.
- You talk or think about being a victim. That can make you want to strike back at someone else.

- You have gotten in trouble for being a bully before.
- You are jealous of other people or their stuff.
- You are moody.
- You don't mind breaking the rules.
- You are in a gang or you are a loner.
- You are cruel to animals or pets.
- You crave attention.
- You are extra competitive.

Another thing a lot of bullies have in common is that they need to feel like they have some power, some control over something (or someone). But there are other ways to feel powerful and important without picking on other kids. Consider these:

- **First, stop your internal dialogue of envy and distrust.** Give yourself some credit for having a good mind, dignity, and the ability to do just about anything you set your mind to. You are never less than anyone unless you put yourself there.
- **Remember what can happen if you don't behave.** Knowing the consequences can stop you from

93

getting into trouble in the first place. Self-control is a kind of power.

· **Resist your payoffs.** You are powerful if you can resist the powerful temptation to do wrong. Say you feel great when you put other kids down because they don't play soccer as well as you. When you brag about your skills and rag on them, calling them names like "scrub," you are being a bully. That's the "crab in a barrel" disease. Crabs stuck in a barrel crawl over other crabs and push them down in order to feel like they are on top. You are a crab in a barrel when you only feel good by putting others down. Doing well makes you powerful; always telling others that they are not as good as you makes you a bully. Resist the temptation to do that.

I don't care how long you've been a bully or how many people you've pushed around. You have the power—and the responsibility—to stop your behavior right now. You aren't a better person for being a bully. You aren't proving your superiority or your smarts or your strength. You aren't going to be better liked because you intentionally refused to invite a girl to your party or because you won't let a smaller kid play soccer with you and your buddies.

You are hurting yourself and other people, and if you want to rediscover the good person you are inside, you have to change your ways. Plus, other kids will be reading this book. And if they apply what I'm telling them here, it's only a matter of time before your bullying days are over anyway.

JOURNAL EXERCISES

- Do I bully anyone? Have I ever bullied someone? Who was it? How did it make me feel?

- What were the payoffs for me for bullying someone? Why was I behaving that way?

- Have I ever stopped bullying someone? Why? Have I been able to make up for the payoff that I got from bullying people? If so, how?

- Who are the kids in my school who I think are being or could be bullied? Why do I think this of them? Is it right for me to take advantage of these reasons?

- Have I ever been punished for bullying someone? If so, by whom?

- Have my friends ever joined in the bullying with me? Have I joined another friend who was acting like a bully? Why?

- Do my parents know I'm a bully? If they did, what would they say? Would they try really hard to make me stop?

ARE YOU A BULLY?

A Quiz

Take this short quiz to find out whether you have any attitudes
that might make you likely to bully another person.

1. You see a friend pushing around another student. What
   do you do?
   a. Join your friend in shoving the student. (5 points)
   b. Watch. (3 points)
   c. Walk away. (2 points)
   *d. Ask another friend or helper to help you find a better
      solution with him or her. (1 point)*

2. A group of popular students invites you to start hanging out with them. One day, while with your new
   friends, you see an old friend who's not as popular.
   One of the popular students dares you to ignore your
   friend when she tries to come up and say hello. How
   do you react?
   *a. Ignore your friend and then laugh at her when she walks
      away. (5 points)*
   *b. Ignore your friend for now and apologize to her later.
      (3 points)*
   c. Say hi to your friend. (2 points)

d. *Say hi to your friend and invite her to sit with you to demonstrate your independence from bullying. (1 point)*

3. You watch while a child takes another child's jacket. How do you handle this?
   a. *Ask the bully to return the jacket. (5 points)*
   b. *Keep walking as if nothing happened. (4 points)*
   c. *Don't say anything but let a trusted adult or teacher know what happened. (3 points)*
   d. *Make a joke about the jacket being taken. (2 points)*
   e. *Call it as it is, and point out the dishonesty and bullying behavior as inappropriate. (1 point)*

4. You and some friends are misbehaving in class and are asked to leave by the teacher. One of your buddies suggests that you and your friends return after school and break the windows of the teacher's classroom. How do you respond?
   a. *Help your friends break the windows. (5 points)*
   b. *Refuse to help. (3 points)*
   c. *Refuse to help, and let an adult know what happened. (2 points)*
   d. *Refuse to help and urge them not to break the windows either. (1 point)*

5. You overhear some people saying mean things about a girl you know. What do you do?

    a. *Come up with mean things of your own to say. (5 points)*

    b. *Ignore them. (3 points)*

    c. *Warn the girl that people are talking about her. (2 points)*

    d. *Tell them to quit talking about the girl. (1 point)*

6. A well-liked guy in school asks you to help him cheat on an English test if you want him to still be your friend. How do you respond?

    a. *Help him cheat. (5 points)*

    b. *Encourage him to do his best on the test without cheating. (4 points)*

    c. *Refuse to be a part. (3 points)*

    d. *Refuse to help and request that the teacher help your friend learn the materials better. (1 point)*

7. You're typing to friends in a chat room one evening when you notice the screen name of a student from school whom you don't like. What do you do?

    a. *Start calling him mean names and posting ugly pictures of him. (5 points)*

    b. *Start to e-mail him, but then decide against causing trouble. (4 points)*

c. Leave it alone and don't respond. *(3 points)*

d. Leave him alone and continue chatting with people you do like. *(1 point)*

8. You walk past the computer lab and notice that the door is unlocked and nobody's in the classroom. Inside is a new laptop. What do you do?

a. Take the laptop. *(5 points)*

b. Walk away. *(4 points)*

c. Shut and lock the door and walk away. *(2 points)*

d. Shut the door and go tell a teacher that the lab was unlocked. *(1 point)*

Scoring Scale

25 points to 40 points—You just might be a bully.

15 points to 24 points—You might not be a bully, but you're not likely to stop one either.

8 points to 14 points—You probably aren't going to be picking on anyone anytime soon.

7

TAKING ON BULLIES: WHAT KIDS CAN DO

TAKING A STAND

I took my time getting to this chapter because I wanted to be sure that I explained the problem of bullying clearly. Once you understand that bullying isn't just about a random physical confrontation, you realize that it usually takes more than a single act to end bullying. You also can see that putting an end to bullying usually takes more than just the victim standing up to a bully.

Still, as I've said before, the person who has the most power to stop a bully is the person the bully targets. It all begins with you. You have to see and believe that you aren't deserving of the threats, the punches, the exclusion, the insults, or the rumors that you have to face. You are not the cause of the bullying, and you certainly do not deserve it. Let me repeat that: You do not deserve it!

But you are the person who is suffering from this bully's behavior. And so, because you love yourself (or are starting to), because you want to be healthy and happy and have every right to be, you have to take the bully on. You have to be willing to do what is necessary to defend yourself, and do so without getting in

trouble or hurting anyone. Just because you are being hurt doesn't make it okay for you to hurt someone else, even a bully. The good news is that you don't have to get yourself in trouble to defend yourself.

There are lots of ways to handle the different types of bullying you might face. We'll get into techniques for dealing with specific kinds of bullies in a minute. First, though, I want to address some of the common ways you can begin to cope with just about any kind of bullying.

I've already mentioned the "Life Laws" I wrote about in my book *Life Strategies for Teens*. In that book, I break down simple ways to live a productive, healthy life for older teens. I'd like to use some of them to help you handle the stresses that come with dealing with bully behavior.

I've said before that you have to "get real" about your situation. The second of my Life Laws basically says that a kid has to remember that he or she creates his or her own experiences. That is to say, you are the person who is most responsible for controlling your life. You have the say over what you will allow to go on and what you won't.

Sure, you may be only a kid. And you still have to place plenty of trust in your mom and dad, your teachers, and other authority figures around you, and they do get a say in what you have to do in a day. But trust me, you still have way more power than you might imagine.

When it comes to bullying, you have to first realize that it can be stopped. Many times kids who are being bullied think that they simply have to take it. They think that no one else cares, that no one notices, or that the bullying will only get worse if they try to stop it. Usually they just don't know what to do.

To think that you have to put up with bullying is negative, and it's untrue. Plenty of people care about you, including your teachers, your parents, your other family members, and your friends—and almost all of them will be able to help you in some way.

You also need to know that this is your life, the one you've been blessed with, and if anyone's going to make it better, it starts with you looking for areas where you can take control. You're not going to magically become the most popular kid or the smartest kid or the biggest kid in school. It takes work and commitment. If you want improvement in your life, you'd better realize that no one has more influence than you over what gets better in your life and why. It may not happen as fast as you like, I'll admit that. But it WILL happen if you work at it and don't quit.

Sometimes kids will try to stand up to a bully once, and their attempt doesn't work. After that, they get frustrated and discouraged and think that the situation is hopeless. They allow the bullying to continue, and it gets worse. Sometimes they try to act as if the bullying isn't that bad, but they know that deep down it hurts them more and more each day. In some cases, they hurt themselves out of desperation. Other times, they explode and attack other people around them senselessly. These are kids who believe they have no control over their lives. They have stopped believing that positive behavior can lead to positive results. So instead of truly trying to save themselves from a bully, they allow themselves to be driven to wrong actions that can end up hurting them or other people.

But in dealing with a bully, you've got to stay positive about being able to end the situation. You have to take a tough look at things you've tried in the past, at what has and hasn't worked. You have to keep going with what is working for you, and you also have to keep trying to come up with new ways of stopping bullies.

Don't stop working at the solutions. Don't let frustration overwhelm you. Your life is too important for you to quit on trying to make it better, especially when it comes to dealing with a bully.

One of the worst effects of being bullied is that it can make you think you deserve to be picked on. But the truth is, you don't have to settle for the role of the bully's target. Even if you're involved in a conflict with a bully, you don't have to buy into the idea that you have to be his or her "victim."

What can you do to rise above this role? Well, let's start by asking a couple of questions. If you don't like the answers to these questions, think about what you can do to change them.

When you see yourself in a mirror, what do you think of yourself? When you examine how you look, how you dress, how you stand or walk, what do you think these things say about you to someone else? Too often, bullies pick on kids who lack self-confidence, who don't feel good about themselves. Kids like this don't think that the rest of the world should like them. When you start to doubt yourself that much, it's even easier for some bully to choose you as his target and reinforce those doubts.

How do you handle yourself around people you don't know well? What kind of impression do you think you leave them with? Are you confident when you talk? Do you speak clearly and make sure they know you are talking? Or do you keep your head down, mumble, and avoid eye contact? If people think that they can dominate you in a conversation or that you won't give much feedback if challenged, they might feel like it'll be easier to get away with outtalking you or doing something else to show that they are somehow "bigger" than you.

How do you handle yourself around friends, classmates, other students, and neighbors? Do you talk freely? Do you listen? Do you make friends easily? Usually bullies like to pick on kids who isolate themselves from other groups. When I was growing up in Dallas, I always made sure I was part of larger groups of kids; I always hung out with a diverse crowd of people. I wasn't everyone's friend, but I was pretty tight with a lot of people. And I certainly had my share of good friends. It's a lot tougher to bully a guy or girl who has even one good friend willing to help out in some way.

Another key in avoiding becoming a bully's target is to remember that you do have control over how people treat you. Friends, enemies, buddies, bullies—all of them deal with you based on your actions and reactions, including what you will and won't let them do. That's the idea at the heart of a couple of other "Life Laws," the ones that say, "We teach people how to treat us" and "People do what works."

I know this may sound silly to some of you and maybe even downright crazy to some others. "C'mon, Jay," you may say. "I'm not LETTING that big ape push me down and steal my lunch money. I didn't teach him to do that. He's doing it because he wants to."

Okay then: Why does he want to? What is he getting out of it?

"My lunch money, man. That and whatever kicks he gets from shoving my face in the dirt at recess."

In other words, the bully who picks on a kid gets some sort of payoff from the behavior. He gets money to buy candy. He gets the emotional satisfaction of feeling like he's in charge of or has control over another person. The bully who verbally abuses someone or drags that person's name through the mud online gets to feel superior, or they think they're showing how they are "funnier" or "cooler." The key, though, is to "teach" these bullies that picking on you no longer "works." We have to remove the payoffs or, if necessary, make picking on you basically not worth it. Right now bullies have been "taught" that they can pick on you and enjoy it. Coming up I am going to give you a plan for making sure that picking on you is no longer fun. We are going to teach them that bullying you, or your friends for that matter, no longer works by eliminating the payoffs they get from being bullies.

There are ways to remove the payoffs that bullies get from the various mean acts they commit, but you have to be willing to recognize things for what they are and accept the reality of the situation. In some cases, kids think it's more trouble to stand up to a bully than it's really worth. They think they aren't being "tough enough" if they let bullying affect them. But that isn't true. Anything that makes you feel bad is worth fixing. And as I said in the introduction, you definitely can't talk about changing a situation until you get real about it.

So try out a few of the principles I've talked about here. Apply them to your everyday relationships with people, especially to any bullies in your life. Remember:

· You are in control of your life.
· You can control how people view and treat you.

· You have to get real about your situation before
you can change it.

FIGHT BACK WITHOUT FIGHTING

For every form that bullying can take, there are effective strategies to act against it. You have many things at your disposal that you can use to help resolve the issue, from your wits to words to support groups. Too often, victims of bullying feel like there's nothing they can do. Maybe they tried to tell someone about the problem before and that person did nothing, leaving the victim feeling like no one cares. Or maybe a victim is too embarrassed to own up to being bullied.

These kinds of experiences can leave you feeling like you have no power to stop the problem. But this isn't true at all. There are ways to resist bullying and stop being a victim. You just have to be willing to give them a real try.

I'm not trying to suggest that all of them will work at all times. There are almost never quick and easy answers to a bully problem. You may have to try different approaches. You may have to create some solutions that fit your individual problem. We'll go into a wide range of things that you can do to stop bullying, by either removing the incentive, standing up for yourself, going to the proper authorities, or enlisting the aid of friends.

But for all the solutions to bullying that you can take, many kids are often tempted to try the one thing you shouldn't do: resort to a bully's tactics. Don't spread rumors about someone else because they've said something mean or untrue about you. Don't start fistfights as a way of combating physical harassment. Don't smear someone online just because he or she has been blasting you in a chat room or in comments on someone's MySpace page.

I know how tempting it can be to get back at someone for hurting you. You want them to feel the same kind of embarrassment and pain—or worse—that they have inflicted on you. But seeking revenge isn't the answer.

There are a couple of good reasons why you shouldn't retaliate against bullies. First of all, you want to bring an end to these actions. Stooping to a bully's level only means you run a greater risk of continuing the bullying—or maybe even making it worse. You don't ever want to seem as though you are fanning the flames of a conflict with a bully.

Secondly, you could get hurt. Many times bullies initiate physical contact with a kid because they are bigger or stronger. That means that, in many cases, they are ready and willing to inflict pain and misery on another kid. Starting a fight with a bully could leave you seriously injured—or worse even. I've heard of some parents telling their kids to "hit him back as hard as you can if he hits you." This isn't good advice, because chances are the bully's going to hit harder.

No, retaliation isn't the answer. And to make sure you don't fly off the handle, there are things you should learn to do to help you cope with the rage and frustration that can come with being bullied.

1. Focus Your Energies

You've got to learn to how to control your feelings when you are being bullied. Getting angry is fine, but you've got keep your anger under control. Flying off the handle can only lead to worse consequences. In recent years, many students who have been bullied have lashed out violently not only at bullies but at other kids around them. Students have been beaten, shot, and killed by kids who have simply grown tired of being picked on day in and day out.

People have all kinds of ways of keeping themselves in check when they want to explode. Some people meditate. They sit for long minutes, trying to clear their minds and calm themselves. Other people have a knack for mentally taking themselves out of a situation, imagining that they are somewhere other than in a conflict with a bully.

Eleven-year-old Eddie says that whenever he had to

face taunting from a neighborhood bully, he imagined himself in a giant glass soundproof booth. "I could see him moving his lips," Eddie says, "but I would imagine that no sound was coming out. He'd be going on about what a bad guy I am, and I'd be sitting there sort of laughing on the inside at how funny he looked with no sound coming out of his mouth. I got really good at going inside my booth. After a while, the guy's big mouth just didn't have any effect on me. I knew I could always tune him out."

Even when the words do reach you, you've got to remember that you're not the person these insults and negative comments make you out to be. That's why I said early on that it's important for you to know your own value. If you know that what someone is saying about you isn't true—if you really believe in yourself deep in your heart—it's going to take a lot more to shake your confidence than just some bully spouting off. Don't let self-doubt creep in where there should be none. Bullies want you to fly off the handle, want to know that they are hurting you in some way. That's a big payoff for many of them. Take the payoff away from them: Stay strong by staying calm.

It's also easier to handle your feelings when you have confidence in yourself. When you know you're good at something, it can alter your attitude and perception. So think about finding activities that can help you seem self-assured in the face of bullying.

One popular activity that has helped former bullying victims is martial arts. Learning self-defense can do wonders for your attitude. Knowing that you can defend yourself can make you more relaxed, less fearful that someone may push you around. I'm not suggesting you take up karate or tae kwon do or some other form of martial arts so that you can hurt someone. Again, fighting is NOT the answer. And in most cases, it's not the martial arts skills that deter bullies, but the confidence that can come with having them.

2. Write Down What You are Feeling

Being bullied stresses many kids out. It forces them to bottle their feelings up inside. You've got to learn healthy, constructive ways to let those feelings out. Even though you have to act like you are in control of your emotions, you cannot afford to act like they aren't there. Really, the opposite is true. To yourself, you have to really look at your emotions from every single angle.

It's okay to acknowledge how bad bullying makes you feel. If you're angry, you have every right to be. If you're sad or hurt, you are entitled to these feelings. Even if you're trying to get over these emotions, you first have to be honest about them if you're going to do anything to make them go away. One good way of letting your feelings out and understanding them is to write them down. Start a journal or a diary. Pour your heart out into its pages. Don't hold anything back. Write honestly about what you're going through, how it makes you feel, and how you want it to stop. Be specific about how you feel, even if you have to really struggle to figure out what those feelings are. Being bullied causes so many feelings all at once that it can be hard to find ways to describe them. But try. It will be worth it.

You don't have to be a great writer—or even good in English class—to keep a journal. Think about ideas and feelings you have and put 'em on paper. You've probably already noticed that at different points in this book there are Journal Exercises, where I want you to write about bullying and how it affects you and other people. If you've never written in a journal before, use these exercises to get yourself started. If you keep a journal, maybe a few of the questions can get you thinking about other feelings you have. But whatever the case, don't hesitate to get your emotions out. We all need to be able to express ourselves.

Here is what Ryan, age thirteen, says:

I never thought much about keeping a diary. I always thought it would be more trouble to write down that stuff than it was worth. Plus, I had plenty of writing to do for class. I just couldn't see how writing more was going to help. But you know what? I was wrong.

I started keeping a journal as part of an English assignment one year. At first I just wrote about a few things that would happen during the day. I always avoided talking too much about how I was feeling.

But then one day, I had a really bad run-in with this group of older kids from a high school near my house. They were always hanging around the school parking lot, picking on smaller kids walking home. They used to scream crazy things at me and would even threaten to run over and pound my face in. On this day, as I was walking by, one of them grabbed my coat out of my hands and tossed it to another big kid. Even though I kept asking them to give it back, they just tossed it back and forth, yelling at me to get it from them as best I could. They kept this up for a long time, until another kid came along and made them give me my jacket.

That afternoon I got home and went straight for my journal. It seemed like I wrote for hours. I just spilled out all my frustrations from that day and all the other days before that I'd had to deal with those guys. I wrote about how bad I felt, how scared of them I was. It took a while, but I found other ways to actually stop them from picking on me. But before I could do that, I needed a way to sort my feelings out, to figure out just what I needed to do. Writing in that journal helped me keep my head clear and helped me sort out how I felt about those guys.

I eventually did a find a way to keep those guys from picking on me. But even before I did, I really appreciated that I was able to let off so much steam just by writing down what I was going through.

Use your thoughts to cleanse yourself emotionally. But don't broadcast your thoughts to take revenge on someone. Don't feel like you need to blast your feelings about a person or a situation into cyberspace or across text messages. When I urge you to write stuff in your diary, it's meant as a personal tool for you to let your feelings flow. It's not meant to be a weapon.

3. Say Good Things About Yourself

Along with writing to yourself, talk to yourself. Go find a mirror, look in it, and say positive things about yourself. Tell yourself all about your best features, your nicest qualities. And be sure to speak the truth. Don't bother saying things that aren't real. All of us have things that we're good at or that we like about ourselves. List some of those traits. Speak them firmly, confidently. Let them sink into your ears, and into your heart.

STRATEGIES FOR TAKING A STAND
SAY NOTHING

More than anything, a kid who's pushing you around or trying to hurt you in other ways wants your attention. It's not enough for some bullies to get other people to take his or her side or to act as if they dislike you. A bully wants

you to notice what he or she is doing and to be scared or wounded by it. He wants to see you cry or stomp off frustrated.

But what happens if you ignore him?

Well, to be honest, in some cases, this may anger a bully even more. This may make the bully want to do even more drastic and harmful things, just to make sure you're "getting the message."

But ignoring him or her just might send a message of your own, one that says you're not buying into the bully's "games" and that you fully intend not to let him or her affect your mood or your behavior. Ignoring a bully is a way of reasserting your control over a situation. It lets him know that he doesn't control you, but rather you have the power to determine how you'll feel and respond.

When you are ignoring him, look directly at him. When he starts mouthing off, just stare at him or her, quiet, stone-faced. Don't try to seem like some tough guy. Just show that you aren't bothered. That too can unsettle bullies, who expect you to acknowledge them in some sort of fearful fashion. A quiet stare lets the bully know that you're not interested in escalating the conflict, but neither are you impressed by his or her antics.

SAY SOMETHING

Even after you address your own feelings, you still have to figure out ways to deal with the actual person who is giving you such a hard time. Talking to yourself is one thing. Talking to a kid who's picking on you on the playground is another, more frightening thing. But you have to be willing to talk.

When you realize that people are trying to bully you, you have to tell them directly that you don't want them picking on you. Let it be known that you aren't going to accept any bullying behavior, that it's not fair, and that you want it to end.

Say some kid's pushing you in the cafeteria line. Don't

hesitate to turn around, look him in the eye, and say in a clear and loud voice, "Stop it! I don't like when you shove me. That's rude."

You just might surprise the guy if you do this. That's because bullies aren't used to kids sticking up for themselves. They want you to suffer quietly. And if you do make any noise, bullies want sobs and whispers, not some loud command to quit screwing with you.

Of course, if you're being bullied, chances are you've wanted to say something to the bully before, but couldn't find the words (or the courage). One reason some children get picked on is precisely because they are not likely to speak up. They are shy, timid, and lacking in confidence. Bullies seek these kinds of kids out. So I realize that speaking up may not be something that you do very well.

But how do you learn to do anything? You practice, practice, practice. Do the same thing I suggested earlier in this chapter about things you can do to better control and express your feelings: Stand in front of the mirror and rehearse what you'll say in given situations.

Think right now about lines that will catch the bully off guard without escalating the situation. The key here is to be prepared. When you are in the heat of the moment, it will be very difficult to think of something to say back, but right now, while it is quiet and there is no stress, you have the opportunity to plan, practice, and be ready to say something in return. And when you are preparing, be ready to use the unexpected. For instance, suppose some kid says to you, "Ha, you've got a big head." You might come back with "Oh, I know already" or "Well, thanks for noticing." Or you can try being more direct. Ask the bully point-blank, "Why are you doing that?" or "What do you really want from me?"

And just as you work on your speech, don't forget to work on your posture, too. Standing tall and looking confident is just as valuable as using the right language to take on a bully. You want to let him or her know that you're not afraid and that you're not interested in taking garbage off of him or her anymore.

It's also helpful to know how to resolve conflicts peacefully when the chance comes up. Sometimes kids endure bullying silently when they are better off using their brains to see if they can solve the problem by working it out directly with whoever they are having issues with. There are three steps you should consider if you're trying to resolve a problem with a bully by talking to him or her:

1. Think about whether the bully believes he or she has a "real" problem with you, based on something you've done or something that he or she thinks you've done.
2. Find out if there's something you can do to solve the problem.
3. See if there's some way you can both decide on a fair outcome.

I realize that talking things out may not necessarily work when dealing with a bully. Some bullies see attempts to talk through a problem as an expression of fear. To some of them, talking is for wimps. But the truth is, talking over a problem is a sign that you're mature, smart, and kind. Sometimes it's worth it for you to try to see if you can work your problems out with words.

SEEK HELP FROM FRIENDS

One big reason bullies can push someone around for a very long time is that kids are sometimes too afraid or embarrassed to tell someone else what's happening to them. But this is just what the bully depends on when giving you a hard time: that they will always get the same scared

reaction from you. So one common way of standing up is to surround yourself with support from other people. It's an old saying: "There's power in numbers."

Fact is, everybody needs friends. Bullies usually try to pick on a kid they know is shy and not very popular. Picking on that kind of victim also makes it easier to get other kids to join in the bullying—or at least not get in the way.

If a bully is pushing you around, try to find kids you can befriend and get involved with them. When I was in school, I always made sure that I was cool with all different groups of students. I played sports, and I had friends in the band and on the cheer team. I had friends from all different walks of life and various age groups.

Learning to create strong, healthy friendships is an important part of life anyway. This is a skill you are going to need even if some bully isn't abusing you. But if you do find yourself being victimized, it helps even more to have friends or to know how to win people over.

Your friends are there to provide support for you. They can tell a bully, "Hey, what you're doing isn't funny or cool. It's stupid, and you should cut it out." They can also help you remember that you're a great person, no matter what someone may have said behind your back or on a website. They can go tell an adult if they see you being attacked. And they can even stand with you to keep a bully from jumping on you or gossiping about you on MySpace. They might be willing to add their voice to yours when you say, "I don't like when you say things that are untrue about me online. Stop."

Don't round up friends to get back at a bully. Don't make friends just so that you can gang up on another kid and strike back. Violence isn't the answer, whether it's just you fighting a bully or you and a group of friends jumping on him or her. Plus, you only encourage the bully to go back, find friends of his own, and return to attack you even more viciously. It's better to find friends who are willing to support you in ways that don't cause more trouble.

Also, if you are being picked on verbally or online, don't try to get back at the other kid by saying or posting mean things about him or her. If you do something like that, you are as wrong as the person you're angry with. And once again, that will probably only make things worse. What you want is for things to get better.

You might also think about befriending an older kid, someone who's kind and doesn't need to feel powerful by pushing around smaller kids. Older kids can be a big help. In some cases, they have gone through what you may be experiencing and can give you some good advice. They might also be willing to walk to or from school with you, introduce you to other kids, and work with the adults in your life to help make sure you stay free from bullying.

WALK (OR RUN) AWAY

One of the most effective ways to handle a bully is to just walk off from the situation. Bullies can't really pick on you if you're not around. If you find yourself being insulted by some girl, just turn and head the other way. If you know some bully's looking to bump into you when you pass his locker, take another route to class. If you know a bully hangs out in a certain hallway at your school or at a particular playground in your neighborhood, steer clear of that place.

Sometimes kids worry about getting called "chicken" or "punk" or even worse names if they are trying to avoid a situation. But avoiding a bullying situation is not being afraid; it's being smart. You don't need to prove anything to anyone by getting yourself in trouble or by being an easy target for some bullies.

And you can also "run" on cyberspace. It may be even easier. Why hang out in a chat room where some kid from school is putting you down all the time? Why go to his Web page just to read mean comments about yourself?

You know that what he says about you doesn't matter, right? You know that you're a whole lot better than he wants to say, right? So don't waste your time going online to read any garbage from someone who doesn't like you or wants to spread lies and gossip.

This doesn't mean that you should live your life in fear, avoiding things you like because a bully will be there. If this becomes the case, then you need to run in the short term, but at the same time, implement another plan that will stop the bullying altogether.

SEVEN TIPS ON HOW NOT TO FIGHT–AND WIN!

· If you have figured out what a bully wants, expose how pitiful the payoff is. If he says to you, "Hey, fatso!" turn to him and ask, "Are you just trying to make yourself look good?"

· Acknowledge the situation frankly or even with laughter: "Oh, so you're going to beat me up again?"

· Help him or her. Sometimes kid bullies just want friends and don't know how to make them. Ask if he or she would rather be a friend than an enemy: "I'm an okay person once you get to know me, and I'll bet you are too."

· Talk about what's going to happen afterward. "C'mon, I don't want to get in trouble with the teacher, and neither do you. So cut it out, okay?"

· Let him or her know that there are always other options: "You don't have to push me. If you want to go by, just let me know and I'll move."

· Bring your resources to the table. Have friends agree to sit down with you and the bully and talk things out.

· Learn how not to get hurt. Remember that you're a worthwhile person and not deserving of anything wrong a bully does to you. Keep this in mind, even while you're working to change the situation in other ways.

CHAPTER SUMMARY
DO'S AND DON'TS OF REACTING TO A BULLY

DO:

- Get real about bullying and how it makes you feel.
- Get angry, but keep your anger under control.
- Write down how you feel.
- Learn to say, and believe, good things about yourself.
- Speak confidently when telling a bully not to physically touch you.
- Work on developing at least one good friendship with a classmate, neighbor, and/or older kid.
- Walk or run away if a bully tries to hurt you.

DON'T:

- Get into a fistfight with a bully or try to retaliate in other ways.
- Believe the insults about you.
- Overestimate how much power a bully has over you.
- Think that bullying will stop if you ignore it.
- Waste time in places online where bullies will target you.
- Be afraid to think of new ways to solve the conflict.
- Believe you deserve to be picked on.

JOURNAL EXERCISES

Have I ever felt challenged by a bully? What were some of the ways the bully tried to hurt me? How did I feel? How did I respond?

- What are some reasons I have to feel good about myself, no matter what some bully may say?

- Who are some friends I have made recently? How did they become my friends and why?

- In what ways do I play the role of a bully victim? When was the last time I did this? Why did I do it? What payoff did I get?

- Have I ever really tried to stop someone from bullying me? What strategies did I try? Did any of them work? Why or why not?

- What other strategies for dealing with a bully can I try that I haven't tried yet? Why haven't I given these a try?

8

NO INNOCENT BYSTANDERS

Okay, so let's say you are fortunate enough not to have to deal with a bully picking on you. You may be big enough or popular enough or just plain lucky enough not to have to deal with someone picking on you in any of the ways we've talked about.

Chances are, you still have a bully problem.

Why? Because you probably know of someone else who is being pushed around or intimidated or taunted over and over again. And that makes it your problem too. This person may be a close friend of yours, your brother or sister,

a teammate, or just someone at school that you don't even know but still see being bullied.

Think about it: Shouldn't everybody at your school or in your neighborhood be able to enjoy himself or herself without having to be afraid of other kids? You wouldn't want someone to shove you into lockers or tease you on the school bus every day. Nobody wants that. And that's why everybody has to make sure that they are working to stamp out bullying.

And don't tell me it can't be done. I've seen young people do some awesome things in recent years to send very clear messages to bullies in their area: We aren't going to put up with you picking on other kids.

You want a great example of how powerful kids can be when they stand up to bullies? Take what happened at a Canadian school in 2007:

A young man at Central Kings Rural High School in Nova Scotia wore a pink polo shirt to school one day. For some reason, this made a few of the bullies around the school very upset. These older boys started picking on the kid, calling him hurtful names, and saying that the pink was girlish, not masculine enough.

Two other students, older boys who had been bullied themselves in years past, heard about what was going on and decided that they weren't going to allow it. The day after learning about the bullying incident, the boys bought fifty pink T-shirts and tank tops. Then they went online and sent out a bunch of e-mails, convincing other students at the school to wear the pink shirts as a show of unity and a protest against bullying.

The boys were flooded with support from friends and classmates. Not only did dozens of other students show up in the shirts, many also came wearing pink from head to toe.

Oh, and the bullies who were picking on that one kid? They never again bothered the kid in the pink shirt—or any other students at the school.

There are a lot of other great examples of kids standing up to bullies as a group, but I wanted to share that one because I think it really proves how effectively kids can act to end bullying. The students at that Canadian school could've looked the other way when they found out about the bullying. They could have joined in or said, "It's not my problem." They didn't. They also didn't wait on teachers or parents to get involved before they did something. And as a result, they managed to make the entire school safe for everyone, regardless of their differences.

It's critical that we take on bullying as communities, rather than just as individuals. I travel the country all the time trying to get kids to agree to work together to stop bullies from making their lives miserable. I've even developed a pledge that students can sign and circulate among other students to sign, as a way of declaring their commitment to stopping bullies. (There's also one for teachers and parents that is included elsewhere in this book.)

I encourage you to look over the pledge and sign it.

Then take it to your school and ask your teachers to help you get it into your school and signed by everyone. And realize that, in doing so, you are joining with thousands of young people all over the country who have agreed to speak out against bullying.

One kid may have a tough time fighting off bullies. But if we all stand together and say loudly that we will not tolerate children being picked on, then together we can make a difference that will benefit everyone's lives.

THE ANTI-BULLYING PLEDGE
FOR STUDENTS

We, the students of _____,
agree to join together to stamp out bullying at our school.

 We believe that everybody should enjoy our school equally and feel safe, secure, and accepted regardless of color, race, gender, popularity, athletic ability, intelligence, religion, or nationality.

Bullying can be pushing, shoving, hitting, and spitting, as well as name-calling, picking on, making fun of, laughing at, and excluding someone. Bullying causes pain and stress to victims and is never justified or excusable as "kids being kids," "just teasing," or any other rationalization. The victim is never responsible for being a target of bullying.

By signing this pledge, we the students agree to:

1. Value student differences and treat others with respect.
2. Not become involved in bullying incidents or be a bully.
3. Be aware of the school's policies and support system with regard to bullying.

4. Report honestly and immediately all incidents of bullying to a faculty member.

5. Be alert in places around the school where there is less adult supervision, such as bathrooms, corridors, and stairwells.

6. Support students who have been or are subjected to bullying.

7. Talk to teachers and parents about concerns and issues regarding bullying.

8. Work with other students and faculty to help the school deal with bullying effectively.

9. Encourage teachers to discuss bullying issues in the classroom.

10. Provide a good role model for younger students and support them if bullying occurs.

11. Participate fully and contribute to assemblies dealing with bullying.

I acknowledge that whether I am being a bully or see someone being bullied, if I don't report or stop the bullying, I am just as guilty.

Signed by: _____

Print name: _____

Date: _____

JOURNAL EXERCISES

Who do I know who is being bullied? Who are some people that I know who would stand up for that person with me?

- What can I do to convince others to stand up against the bullies too?
- Do I care if a stranger is being bullied? Why should I care?
- What will I do the next time I see a kid being bullied?
- What can I do to get my schoolmates to sign an anti-bullying pledge?
- What can my friends and I do to help our school come up with and enforce an anti-bullying policy?

EDUCATING PARENTS

Now that you have learned so much about bullying and the new ways kids bully one another, such as online bullying, you probably know more about how to stop today's bullies than your parents do. You can use all of the information you've learned here to help your parents understand bullies and your feelings about them. Your parents are important people to have on your side. Think of them as your body-guards. You now have the power—this information—to help them so they can help you.

A lot of times when parents find out that their children

have been bullied, the parents tell the kids to fight back. That's something you probably don't want to hear when you are the one who has to come face-to-face or toe-to-toe with a bully. Let's face it, whether you are the bully, the target, or a bystander, there are a few other reasons you may not want to talk to your parents about the situation.

· You are ashamed of your behavior.
· You don't think your parents will be any help.
· You don't want to get into trouble.

All of these reasons are understandable. What you need to do is find a way to start a conversation with your parents so that you can begin to teach them what you've learned here.

Where do you begin? Be open with your parents, so they open their ears to what you want to teach them.

Chances are your parents don't have a clue about how kids bully one another today, and they may not remember all of the run-ins they had with bullying when they were young. One good way to start the conversation is to just ask your parents if you can be their helper. Tell them that you've read up on the subject of bullies, and there are some things you saw in the book that they should know. Parents love that sort of positive stuff. It helps you sound like you know what you're talking about when you can quote books. Plus, it's a smooth way to ease into what could be a tough talk.

Once you have their attention, then you let them know about your situation with bullies or your opinions. Here are the topics you want to cover with your parents.

ASK FOR THEIR HELP

I've always told kids that when you cut your parents in on your problem, they will have to take some responsibility for solving it. But if you don't say anything, you can't be mad at them for not doing anything to help. Remember, they may not notice the warning signs. After you describe your bully problem, tell them that you want them to have a zero tolerance for bullying. Yes, tell them that means they need to call the bullies' parents and visit the school to talk to the teachers and the principal to make sure that they are not

allowing the bullying either. Remember, you're not a tattle-tale. Your parents are on your side, just like the bully's parents are probably going to be on his or her side. Your parents can't "have your back" unless you tell them what's up.

If this talk is the first time your parents are hearing about your bully problem, the chat can get long. They're going to ask a lot of questions. They may even feel dumb or angry with themselves for not knowing. But don't get so carried away with the discussion that you forget to teach your folks the best ways they can help you. Whether you are a victim or a bully, tell your parents you need them to listen to you, believe in you, and be people you can count on for help.

Try saying this; it should work: "I need you to help me to be myself, respect myself, and protect myself."

Y'all may think it's awkward or difficult to "teach" your parents this way. They may not be good listeners. Or you may feel like you are lecturing (boring!). An easy way to get them to listen is to first get them talking about themselves and their childhood. Ask Dad how he dealt with bullies when he was growing up. As your parents tell their stories, point out the differences between bullies then and bullies now. For example, when Dad starts to tell you about how his bully, Henry, used to punch him and steal his lunch money in sixth grade, remind him that bullies don't always beat up people anymore. Dad may give you a confused look. That's because for your parents, and the generations before them, bullying equaled beatings.

Here's a list to pass on to your folks. Parents, teachers, and counselors can teach you these skills to make you bullyproof:

· Respect for other people's feelings
· Hope

- Bravery
- Self-control
- Self-motivation
- Anger management

CONFESS

If you are a bully, or someone who stood by and didn't do anything when someone was being bullied, now is the time to come clean. Tell your parents to contact the victim's parents for you. It may help to ease the hard feelings if you go to the victim together to apologize.

TEACH THE WARNING SIGNS

Teach your folks how to identify the warning signs of bullying—for your sake and for the sake of your brothers, sisters, and other kids in your community.

Here are a couple of stories to share with your parents to show them what can happen when parents don't notice the warning signs of bullying.

Bobby's parents thought he was just experiencing the difficulties of getting used to a new school in a new city. It all began during his first week of school in Fremont, California. At first the seventh grader couldn't wait to take the bus. He figured he would get in good with the cool kids who sat at the back. But that's where Todd sat. Todd was a tall, skinny eighth grader who all the parents liked because he was a great Little League soccer player.

Every day when Bobby got on the bus, Todd would tell the other kids that new kids were "nobodies." So since everyone wanted to be cool like Todd, nobody wanted to sit next to Bobby. Pretty soon Bobby would get up for school late every day so his mom would have to drive him. Problem solved, right? Wrong. Todd waited for Bobby in the bathroom between classes and stripped him of his lunch money. Within a month, Bobby had stomachaches from not eating lunch and from

"holding it" all day. He wouldn't hang out with other kids at the mall because he had given Todd all his money. Bobby became a loner.

Eventually Bobby stopped going to school and sat in a park every day, trying to figure out how to deal with Todd. Bobby figured he could make friends with Todd if he made the soccer team. That only made Todd's torture worse. He and his buddies told Bobby that he had to show he was tough before he could make the team. After the first day of tryouts, Todd hit Bobby in the head with a soccer ball sixty-four times. Bobby was hospitalized with a concussion (a bruise on the brain). He told his mom he fell at tryouts. Two days later Bobby convinced his mom to let him go back to Oregon to live with his dad. His grades had dropped to all Ds.

There were lots of warning signs that Bobby was a victim of bullying. Work together with your parents to identify ten warning signs.

Remember to stress to parents that bullying does *not* have to involve violence. Everybody—boys, girls, and very young children—can be involved in emotional bullying by teasing, hurting each other's feelings, and using threats. Sometimes the threat of violence can have the same effect as violence on a victim's mind and spirit. Tell your parents they need to be on the lookout for bullying, even when nobody gets beat up.

One day Kelly, my BFF in fourth grade, told me that she wouldn't be my friend anymore unless I let her have my Cheetah Girls necklace. She said she should have it since she was prettier. After a while she started to insult me in front of everybody, saying stuff like, "I heard you went to the haunted house and they offered you a job," and "I thought about you today—I was at the zoo." She said if I asked her for the necklace back again she was going to wring my neck with it. I'm usually shy, but I got sick of it and started practicing my comebacks by dissing my four-year-old sister. I told her she had better not tell, but she did. My mother got on my case. I blew up at her. I couldn't talk to my mom about Kelly because I figured it was Mom's fault I was so ugly.
—Mackenzie, age ten, New York

Mackenzie showed classic signs of verbal bullying. Can you and your parents put your heads together to come up with at least eight?

Okay, now you know how to educate your parents. Remember, the whole point is to team up with them, because it is their job to empower you. The last step to schooling your parents is to get them to sign on the dotted line. Get them to take the Pledge.

ANTI-BULLYING PLEDGE
FOR PARENTS

This anti-bullying parents' pledge is a promise parents can make to remind them to help children fight bullying without violence.

We, the parents of _____, agree to join together to stamp out bullying at our school.

We believe that everybody should enjoy our school equally and feel safe, secure, and accepted regardless of color, race, gender, popularity, athletic ability, intelligence, religion, or nationality.

Bullying can be pushing, shoving, hitting, and spitting, as well as name-calling, picking on, making fun of, laughing at, and excluding someone. Bullying causes pain and stress to victims and is never justified or excusable as "kids being kids," "just teasing," or any other rationalization. The victim is never responsible for being a target of bullying.

By signing this pledge, we the parents agree to:

1. Keep ourselves and our children informed and aware of school bullying policies.

2. Work in partnership with the school to encourage positive behavior, valuing differences, and promoting sensitivity to others.

3. Discuss regularly with our children their feelings about schoolwork, friendships, and relationships.
4. Inform faculty of changes in our children's behavior or circumstances at home that may change a child's behavior at school.
5. Alert faculty if any bullying has occurred.

Signed by: _____

Print name: _____

Date: _____

JOURNAL EXERCISES

- What took me so long to talk to my parents about my bully problem?
- Do I really believe that my parents can help me? What do I want them to do?
- What do I know about bullies that I can teach my parents?
- Do I trust that my parents will do the right thing to solve my problem? Why or why not?
- Why should my parents step in to help me?

10
WHAT KIDS CAN ASK SCHOOLS TO DO

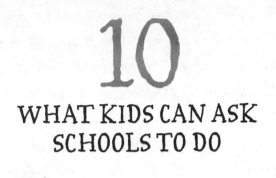

Lisa picks on Kellie almost every day at school, but she always makes sure she does it when no adults are around. She pulls Kellie's hair, steals her pencils, and knocks her folders off her desk when she walks by.

One day while they are in gym class, Lisa walks by Kellie and throws her arms out like she's yawning. Her elbow catches Kellie in the nose and makes it bleed. Lisa grabs Kellie's arm, drags her into a nearby bathroom, and stuffs tissue up her nose, hoping to stop the bleeding before anyone else shows up.

Fortunately, Ms. Berger, a math teacher, happens to notice

Lisa rush by with Kellie and becomes suspicious. She is one of the few teachers who has noticed that Lisa isn't very nice to Kellie. So she excuses herself from her math class and follows the girls to the bathroom. She walks in just as Lisa is threatening to hurt Kellie if she tells anyone what happened to her nose.

Ms. Berger isn't afraid, of course. She cleans Kellie's nose and sends her to the school nurse. Then she marches Lisa right into the principal's office. Lisa winds up getting suspended from school.

Ms. Berger also begins to work with other kids to find out more about how bad bullying is at the school. She is shocked to find out that kids like Lisa push their classmates around all day long.

Within months she has convinced the principal to do more to cut down on bullying at the school. He had no idea that the problem was as bad as it was. Pretty soon, though, word gets around: Any kid caught picking on another would be tossed out.

Not everything gets better overnight, but pretty soon the bullies have gotten the message, and so have their victims: This school is going to be safe for everybody.

As I've been saying throughout this book, you shouldn't have to feel like you're up against a bully alone. And just as you have your parents and good friends who can help you with a bully problem, you should also be able to look to the adults who run your school for help. The fact is, most bullying cases happen in or around schools. This means that teachers, principals, and other adults at your school are the grown-ups who are closest to what's going on. You need to know that you can depend on them to make school safe for you and for everyone else. School authorities don't like bullying any more than parents and other adults do. So don't be afraid to reach out to them for help when you are facing a bully. They are the ones who can usually take the most immediate and direct action.

Many kids are reluctant to talk to teachers and other faculty because they don't want to be accused of ratting out another kid. We've all been taught that getting someone

in trouble by squealing on them isn't nice and isn't very mature. "Don't be a tattletale" is what moms and dads often say. However, your parents and other adults do want you to let them know when there is a potentially dangerous situation brewing. And it pays for you to know the difference.

Tattling is usually done just to make trouble for another child. If you're reporting someone's behavior just to get that person in trouble, you're probably tattling. However, if you are letting an adult know about a situation that, if not handled, could lead to trouble or danger, then you're doing the right thing in opening your mouth.

So overhearing Larry swearing might not be worth running to find the principal about. However, if you overhear Larry swearing at another student and threatening to hurt the kid, then you should let someone know right away that Larry is behaving like a bully.

Obviously, one of the biggest ways that adults at school can help is by stepping in to stop a bully from picking on you or someone else. You can help them with this by letting them know the areas of your school where the bullies hang out and where they often pick on their victims. In many instances, it's a bathroom or a back hall or a part of a playground. So be sure that your teachers know what places they especially need to keep an eye on, so they can be ready to step in when problems come up.

But there are other reasons you should seek out help from the school staff if you really want to reduce bullying. Here are six reasons why bringing adults at school into the mix is a good idea:

1. The staff supervises.

Principals, teachers, aides—these people have been asked to keep control over what happens at the school. They run the school, not the bullies and cliques. They are the people who have been trained to handle certain situations, and many of them have a lot of experience dealing with taunting, harassment, verbal attacks, and even physical abuse among students. It's important that you respect their authority. You show this respect by helping them maintain order at school. You're also letting people know that you understand how authority works at the school and that bullies aren't in charge.

2. Teachers can set rules.

If there's a problem with bullies at your school, principals and teachers can come up with different ways to tackle the situation. Certainly one of the first steps might be to make bullying against the rules at your school. Students who are caught doing it to others might be seriously punished.

Also, there are many programs and policies, like the anti-bullying pledge, that teachers can use to educate students about the negative effects of bullying. If the staff starts to think that bullying is a big problem at your school, they have the power to call assemblies, create classes, and make up policies that can reduce the harassment.

3. Principals and teachers can talk with other students.

If you talk to adults at some schools, they'll tell you that they don't know about any bullying going on. But if you talk to the kids, they'll tell you a very different story. They see bullying going on around them and don't think the adults are doing enough to stop it.

But before your principal can do something about it, he or she has to know what's really going on, right? And that means that the principal needs to be able to talk to you and to your friends and classmates about how they are being treated at school. But sometimes students are not willing to talk to teachers and other people on the staff. Maybe you don't think you can trust them. Or maybe you think they don't care. I can't say for sure if you're wrong about both of these ideas. But I'll tell you that you need to try.

And many times, when one student approaches a teacher or principal, that person will do his or her best to work out the situation. And that may involve sitting down with the other kid to try to work out the problem. Okay, so you might be afraid to go to that big fifth grader and ask him to sit down and talk about his problems with you. But when the vice principal shows up, it's another story! She has ways of making him talk. And adults can also act like the umpire in a baseball game when handling a talk between two kids: They can let you know when you're being fair, when you can't interrupt, and when you have made a very good point.

4. Adults can work with other adults.

If kids at school are harassing you, your principal and teachers can reach out to other adults to help you solve the problem. That might mean going to a counselor to help you talk about your feelings. Or a teacher talking with other teachers about keeping an ear out for nasty gossip in and around their classrooms. Or the principal talking to the school security chief about increasing patrols around the schoolyard.

5. Adults can keep your parents aware.

Maybe it's not easy for you to tell your dad that you're being

picked on at school or online by some classmates. Maybe it'd be easier if you told someone at school and asked if they could help you tell your folks. Talking with adults can provide you with someone more experienced and more mature to help you talk through the situation with Mom and Dad. Perhaps they could work with you to come up with the right words to say. Or maybe they could sit with you and your parents as you talk it out.

6. School staff sets the tone.

Adults can send a very powerful message that bullying won't be tolerated at your school. They certainly can punish the

160

bullies who pick on weaker kids. But they can also come up with ways to work with the bullies to try to straighten out their behavior. Instead of just tossing out kids who bully or throwing them in detention, teachers and principals can reward students who work to stop bullying. There might be prizes or trips or other cool gifts for kids who help let it be known that bullying is not going to be allowed.

As part of setting that tone, I've included another pledge for schools that are interested in doing something to put an end to bullying in their classrooms, hallways, and playgrounds. Maybe you can pass it along to someone in charge at your school as a way of helping to make it a better place to learn and grow.

ANTI-BULLYING PLEDGE
FOR SCHOOLS

We, the faculty of _____,
agree to join together to stamp out bullying at our school.

We believe that everybody should enjoy our school equally
and feel safe, secure, and accepted regardless of color, race,
gender, popularity, athletic ability, intelligence, religion, or
nationality.

Bullying can be pushing, shoving, hitting, and spitting,
as well as name-calling, picking on, making fun of, laughing
at, and excluding someone. Bullying causes pain and stress
to victims and is never justified or excusable as "kids being
kids," "just teasing," or any other rationalization. The victim
is never responsible for being a target of bullying.

By signing this pledge, we the school and faculty agree to:

1. Develop a clear school policy on bullying and display
   it prominently in classrooms and around the school.

2. Train faculty in appropriate handling of incidents.

3. Develop or adopt a curriculum that educates students
   about bullying.

4. Teach students about less obvious forms of bullying,
   like gossiping and exclusion.

5. Discuss proactive anti-bullying measures (such as having
   lunch with a student who has been excluded in the past).

6. Establish support systems for pupils involved in incidents, such as peer counseling and mediation.
7. Establish a system to inform and support parents when incidents of bullying occur.
8. Offer counseling to students who bully.
9. Ensure an atmosphere where students feel safe reporting incidents of bullying and confident they will be dealt with and not ignored.
10. Report all incidents of bullying immediately to the principal.
11. When an incident is reported, all students involved will be given the opportunity to give their version of the incident.
12. Put in place sanctions for bullying such as verbal warnings, removal from a classroom or school grounds, a verbal or written apology to the victim, a parent-teacher meeting, and detention or expulsion for repeat offenders.
13. Monitor cases of persistent bullying and be fully informed of all incidents and their progress.

Signed by: _____

Print name: _____

Date:_____

JOURNAL EXERCISES

- Is my school safe for me and other kids? What has happened at school that might make me think it's not as safe as it should be? What more would I like to see the school staff do to keep us safe from bullies?

- Who are the adults at my school who I trust? Who I can talk to about bullying in my life or bullying that I have witnessed?

- Do I need them to talk to my parents for me as well?

- Why haven't I talked to the school staff before now? Am I over those fears or do I need to get some of my friends to go and talk to the school staff with me?

- Are there some places around my school that my school staff should pay attention to in order to cut down on the bullying in our school?

11
FORGIVING A BULLY

Jeremy used to get bullied as a kid. A boy at his elementary school used to push and kick him. When they were on the playground, the boy never let Jeremy play in any of the games. He'd threaten to hurt Jeremy if he even touched the ball.

Several years later Jeremy saw the bully on the street. As soon as he did, all the memories of how the boy used to treat him came back to him, and Jeremy got angry. Older, and now bigger and taller than the boy who used to pick on him, Jeremy walked over to the ex-bully and looked him in the eye. "I should punch you in your face for all you used to do to me," Jeremy said *angrily. The bully bows his head for a moment and then looks up at Jeremy with sadness in his eyes. "I'm sorry for the things I used to do," he says. "I was an angry kid with a lot of pain. But I joined a church and began studying about God, and I have learned why what I did was wrong. I'm a youth minister now. I understand that I hurt you. And I'm very sorry."*

Jeremy was so shocked he didn't know what to say. He didn't want to punch the young man anymore. But those memories wouldn't leave him. And neither could the anger they created. Jeremy sputtered something under his breath and walked off, the pain of those years as a frightened victim still in his heart.

The pain that Jeremy felt is something that many of us have to deal with. It's the sort of pain that lasts in your heart even after you've gotten over the physical scars on your body. As we've seen, the effects of bullying can last forever and can ruin your life or someone else's if you're not careful. Even after you've grown up or moved away from the bully, you will still have to deal with the feelings that come with being pushed around: anger, powerlessness, lack of hope, fear, and other emotions.

That's why it's important that you learn how to forgive people when they hurt you. I'm not saying it's easy all the time, because I know that it's not. I'm not going to tell you that it's something you'll be able to do right away, because sometimes it takes a while to learn to honestly forgive someone who has hurt you.

But I want you to realize also that you have to learn to forgive, not just for the bully's sake, but because it will do you good and make you feel better. Real forgiveness can make you feel free. It can release you from the sadness and the frustration and the anger that come with being bullied by someone. It paves the way for you to become a better person.

How does it do this? Well, forgiveness is about letting go of the hurt. When you don't forgive, you keep the pain of being bullied bottled up inside of you. That pain can lead to other problems:

It can make you not want to be a part of a group with others. When people feel embarrassed, they don't want to be around others because they worry that they will be

167

laughed at. When you allow yourself to continue to live with the scars of bullying, you run the risk of losing out on other good times with good people in your life by not spending time with them.

It can make you mean and not trusting of others. You can begin to think of everyone as a possible bully (or worse, as a victim who you can push around). In this case, you find yourself not believing in people when they tell you good things about yourself or about how they feel about you. You're more worried about getting hurt than you are about building strong friendships.

It can make you not want to feel anything at all. Often, kids who get pushed around try to hide their feelings and act as if nothing bothers them. They begin to lie to themselves about how they feel and even about whether they feel any emotions. You can become confused about feelings and try to force yourself not to show anything. But keeping your feelings bottled up this way—or trying to pretend you don't have any feelings—will only add to your stress and pain.

Sure, you can blame the pain on the bully, and that's true. If he or she hadn't gossiped about you online or left you out of the schoolyard games or shoved you down every day, you wouldn't be feeling hurt.

But once you've handled the bullying and gotten it to stop, then you have to also get past the pain that came along with it. If you don't do this, then you are letting the past still hurt you. You have stopped the bullying, but you are still letting the bully beat you in other ways. The bully still controls your mind and your feelings. You should never, ever give anyone the power to do this to you. And the way you stop it is by learning to forgive people.

Now, I'm not saying that you shouldn't want what's fair just because you forgive. If a bully has been bothering you, you have to first get him or her to stop hurting you. If someone has mistreated you, stolen your things, or hurt you in other ways, it's not wrong to want to see that person punished for what he or she did to you. Personally, I think that bullies usually get what's coming to them one way or another—and they should. They pay a high price for how they act toward other kids.

But just knowing that a bully got in trouble is still not enough to remove the pain that he or she may have caused you. Even if the bully apologizes, it may not change anything. You have to be able to forgive that person before you can truly get over what has happened. You also don't want the pain and anger to affect other relationships that you have. You don't want to find yourself taking your problems out on people who have not hurt you. Forgiving someone makes you better able to put the pain that he or she caused behind you and move on with your life.

Forgiveness doesn't mean that you've forgotten about what someone has done to you. And it doesn't mean that you have to let that bully, or anyone else, hurt you again. Forgiveness is just you saying to yourself that you are no longer going to let feelings created by something that happened in the past ruin your present and your future. Forgiveness isn't just about you doing something kind for a bully.

Forgiveness is also about you doing something good for yourself. Forgiveness can be your most effective tool if you're ever going to beat bullies once and for all.

JOURNAL EXERCISES

- Why is it important to forgive a bully? Do I think I could do it? Why or why not?
- Who have I bullied that I need to apologize to and ask to forgive me?
- Is it important that someone who bullied me apologize for it? Can I forgive the bully (or the bystanders) even if they do not apologize?
- How can I benefit from forgiving a bully?
- What are some ways that I can hurt myself by not forgiving a bully?
- What's wrong with getting revenge instead of forgiving the bully?

ACKNOWLEDGMENTS

First and foremost, thank you to my wife, Erica. You make me happier than I ever thought possible and I feel so lucky to be married to you. You have contributed to this book more than anyone will ever know, and your passion about this topic is an inspiration. Your love, friendship, and energetic spirit make each and every day all I could have ever wanted. I respect you, admire you, and am blessed by the light you bring to my life.

I would like to sincerely thank my dad for always believing in and supporting me. Thanks, Dad, for never being too busy, too tired, or too distracted. You make me proud to be your son and inspire me to be a better person. You are always excited to help and we always have fun in the process. Thanks for everything, Dad—I love you.

Heartfelt thanks to my mom for being in my corner no matter what I am doing. You hold our family together. Thanks, Mom—I love you.

Thanks to my brother, Jordan, who keeps me laughing constantly and always encourages me. You make me extremely proud—I love you.

I would like to thank Darrell Dawsey for believing in this project and putting in the extra effort to make sure it happened. The amazing work that you contributed to this book and your positive attitude are greatly appreciated.

It is such a privilege to work with the best of the best, and Steve Björkman's illustrations brought this book to life. Thank you for your contribution and for always bringing your A game to the process.

Thank you also to Frank Lawlis for his contribution to this project and for his friendship. Frank, you too made such an enormous contribution to this book that it absolutely would not have been the same without you. Thanks for everything, Frank.

Thanks to "Uncle Scott" Madsen for all that you do to help and support me in everything that I do. You certainly make it all more fun!

Thanks to Mark McVeigh, my editor at Aladdin. You have made this project the best it could be and your editorial direction has made this a better book. Thank you too to Alyson Heller for her contribution. My sincere appreciation and thanks also goes to Rick Richter, president of S&S juvenile division, for believing in the vision and being committed to getting this book in the hands of every parent, teacher, and child who is dealing with this challenge on a daily basis.

Special thanks to Lucille Rettino and her great marketing team, and Paul Crichton and his great publicity team at S&S,

and also to publishers Bethany Buck, Ellen Krieger, Rubin Pfeffer, and Mara Anastas.

Jan Miller and Dupree/Miller & Associates—I quite literally would not be doing this without you. You not only make it possible but you also make it fun. Thank you, Jan, for being such an amazing supporter and friend!

And an enormous thank-you to Shannon Marven: you are amazing. The behind-the-scenes work that you do has improved the lives of millions of Americans, and I would like to thank you on behalf of them all. There are no others like you. I personally appreciate your dedication and hard work more than you will ever know. Thank you!